16⁹⁹

Your Happy Healthy Pet™

Boxer

2nd Edition

GET MORE!
Visit www.wiley.com/
go/boxer

Stephanie Abraham

FRANKLIN SQ. PUBLIC LIBRARY
19 LINCOLN RO
FRANK

This book is printed on acid-free paper.

Copyright © 2008 by Wiley Publishing, Inc., Hoboken, New Jersey. All rights reserved.

Howell Book House
Published by Wiley Publishing, Inc., Hoboken, New Jersey

No part of this publication may be reproduced, stored in a retrieval system or transmitted in any form or by any means, electronic, mechanical, photocopying, recording, scanning or otherwise, except as permitted under Sections 107 or 108 of the 1976 United States Copyright Act, without either the prior written permission of the Publisher, or authorization through payment of the appropriate per-copy fee to the Copyright Clearance Center, 222 Rosewood Drive, Danvers, MA 01923, (978) 750-8400, fax (978) 646-8600, or on the web at www.copyright.com. Requests to the Publisher for permission should be addressed to the Legal Department, Wiley Publishing, Inc., 10475 Crosspoint Blvd., Indianapolis, IN 46256, (317) 572-3447, fax (317) 572-4355, or online at http://www.wiley.com/go/permissions.

Wiley, the Wiley logo, Howell Book House, the Howell Book House logo, Your Happy Healthy Pet, and related trade dress are trademarks or registered trademarks of John Wiley & Sons, Inc. and/or its affiliates in the United States and other countries, and may not be used without written permission. All other trademarks are the property of their respective owners. Wiley Publishing, Inc. is not associated with any product or vendor mentioned in this book.

The publisher and the author make no representations or warranties with respect to the accuracy or completeness of the contents of this work and specifically disclaim all warranties, including without limitation warranties of fitness for a particular purpose. No warranty may be created or extended by sales or promotional materials. The advice and strategies contained herein may not be suitable for every situation. This work is sold with the understanding that the publisher is not engaged in rendering legal, accounting, or other professional services. If professional assistance is required, the services of a competent professional person should be sought. Neither the publisher nor the author shall be liable for damages arising here from. The fact that an organization or Website is referred to in this work as a citation and/or a potential source of further information does not mean that the author or the publisher endorses the information the organization or Website may provide or recommendations it may make. Further, readers should be aware that Internet Websites listed in this work may have changed or disappeared between when this work was written and when it is read.

For general information on our other products and services or to obtain technical support please contact our Customer Care Department within the U.S. at (800) 762-2974, outside the U.S. at (317) 572-3993 or fax (317) 572-4002.

Wiley also publishes its books in a variety of electronic formats. Some content that appears in print may not be available in electronic books. For more information about Wiley products, please visit our web site at www.wiley.com.

Library of Congress Cataloging-in-Publication Data:
Abraham, Stephanie.
    Boxer / Stephanie Abraham. — 2nd ed.
       p.   cm.
    Includes index.
    ISBN 978-0-470-22182-2
    1. Boxer (Dog breed)   I. Title.
    SF429.B75A37   2008
    636.73—dc22   2008001351

Printed in the United States of America

10 9 8 7 6 5 4 3 2 1

Book design by Melissa Auciello-Brogan
Cover design by Michael J. Freeland
Book production by Wiley Publishing, Inc. Composition Services

About the Author

Stephanie Abraham grew up with a Boxer named Duchess in the 1950s. When she married her husband, David, in 1969 they quickly purchased a Boxer puppy who grew up to be American and Canadian Ch. Gray Roy's Minstrel Boy, LOM. Since then, breeding under the kennel name Trefoil, they have bred and/or owned more than fifty AKC champions.

Stephanie has judged the breed since 1982 and has been all over the world on her judging assignments, including Australia, Japan, Britain, and Brazil. She has written the Boxer column in the *AKC Gazette* for more than fifteen years and is head of publicity and judges' education for the American Boxer Club. She is American Boxer Club delegate to the AKC. Her award-winning book, *The Boxer: Family Favorite,* has been a source of great pride.

David and Stephanie live in rural Connecticut with their Boxers, several Cavalier King Charles Spaniels, and four very tolerant cats.

About Howell Book House

Since 1961, Howell Book House has been America's premier publisher of pet books. We're dedicated to companion animals and the people who love them, and our books reflect that commitment. Our stable of authors—training experts, veterinarians, breeders, and other authorities—is second to none. And we've won more Maxwell Awards from the Dog Writers Association of America than any other publisher.

As we head toward the half-century mark, we're more committed than ever to providing new and innovative books, along with the classics our readers have grown to love. From bringing home a new puppy to competing in advanced equestrian events, Howell has the titles that keep animal lovers coming back again and again.

Contents

Shopping List

You'll need to do a bit of stocking up before you bring your new dog or puppy home. Below is a basic list of some must-have supplies. For more detailed information on the selection of each item below, consult chapter 5. For specific guidance on what grooming tools you'll need, review chapter 7.

- ☐ Food dish
- ☐ Water dish
- ☐ Dog food
- ☐ Leash
- ☐ Collar
- ☐ Crate

- ☐ Nail clippers (scissors or guillotine type)
- ☐ Soft curry brush
- ☐ Chew toys (tough nylon "bones" that cannot be destroyed)
- ☐ ID tag for collar

There are likely to be a few other items that you're dying to pick up before bringing your dog home. Use the following blanks to note any additional items you'll be shopping for.

☐ _____

☐ _____

☐ _____

☐ _____

☐ _____

☐ _____

☐ _____

☐ _____

☐ _____

☐ _____

☐ _____

☐ _____

Pet Sitter's Guide

We can be reached at (___)_____-_____ Cell phone (___)_____-_____

_____

We will return on _____ (date) at _____ (approximate time)

Dog's Name _____

Breed, Age, and Sex _____

Important Names and Numbers

Vet's Name _____ Phone (___)_____-_____

Address _____

Emergency Vet's Name _____ Phone (___)_____-_____

Address _____

Poison Control _____ (or call vet first)

Other individual (someone the dog knows well and will respond to) to contact in case of emergency or in case the dog is being protective and will not allow the pet sitter in. _____

_____

Care Instructions

In the following three blanks let the sitter know what to feed, how much, and when; when the dog should go out; when to give treats; and when to exercise the dog.

Morning _____

_____

Afternoon _____

_____

Evening _____

_____

Medications needed (dosage and schedule) _____

_____

Any special medical conditions _____

_____

Grooming instructions _____

_____

My dog's favorite playtime activities, quirks, and other tips_____

_____

_____

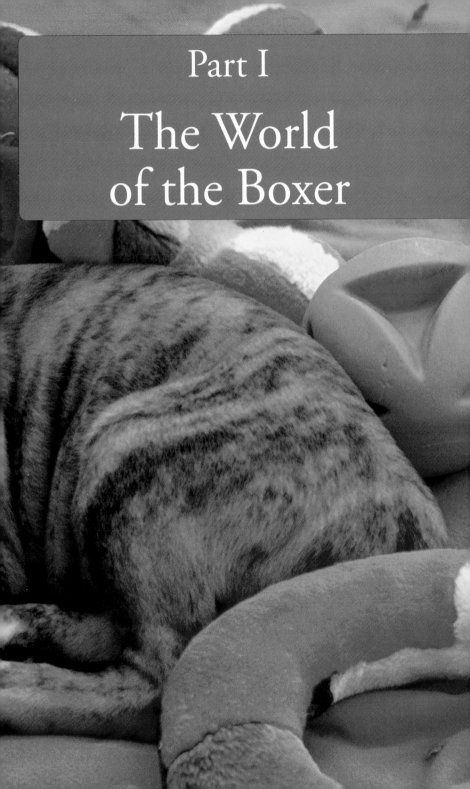

Part I
The World of the Boxer

The Boxer

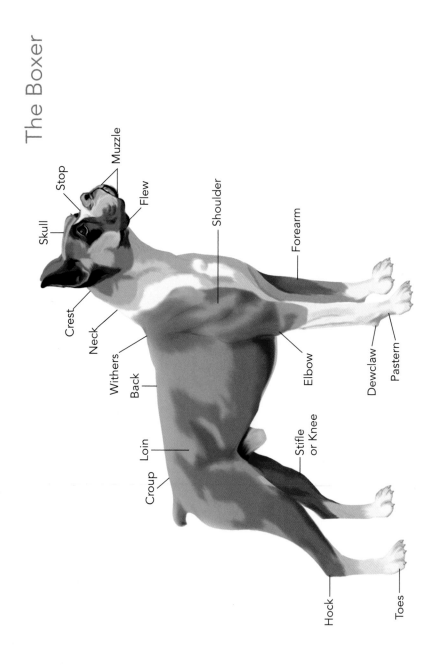

- Muzzle
- Stop
- Skull
- Flew
- Shoulder
- Forearm
- Crest
- Neck
- Withers
- Back
- Elbow
- Dewclaw
- Pastern
- Loin
- Croup
- Stifle or Knee
- Hock
- Toes

Chapter 1

What Is a Boxer?

Congratulations! You have decided to share your life with a Boxer, one of the most engaging breeds in dogdom. I hope the following chapters will help you to understand your Boxer and to care for him so that you live a long and happy life together.

He will return all the love and affection you give—and then some. He will protect you, he will make you laugh on the darkest days, and he will outwit you when he feels the need. His loyalty will astonish you, his energy will exhaust you, and his devotion will always be constant.

The Essence of the Boxer

A Boxer is a complicated animal. More than any other dog, his moods mirror those of his master. His sensitivity is astonishing. While he is a great clown, always ready to run and play, he can display great courage and even aggression when needed. His eyes are almost human in their expression, and in them you can clearly read his state of mind.

A dog with these sensitivities is no wind up toy; he is not an animal who can always be counted on to do what is expected. He is not a dog for everyone, and if you're thinking about getting a Boxer, you must decide whether the characteristics of the breed will appeal.

The Boxer is often the very definition of "independence." While he may mellow with age, a Boxer is a physically active dog. He loves to roughhouse—he will fetch an object and cheerfully dare you to take it back. He will refuse to move over if you attempt to push him aside. He has a tendency to jump up, and there is considerable muscular force behind these loving greetings.

This agile leaping is no doubt a part of his genetic heritage: His name derives from the German word *boxen,* which, of course, means "boxer." Although it cannot be definitely proven, the name probably derives from the Boxer's habit of playing with his front paws. He uses these paws almost like hands—to poke, to punch, and, after giving birth, to cradle puppies.

One cannot underestimate a Boxer's strength. He is quite capable of knocking an adult man to his knees. It is therefore imperative to train a Boxer to curb his natural tendencies to leap and make body contact. Remember, he was bred to overpower large animals (more about that in chapter 2), so these instincts come quite naturally to your Boxer. Happily, he has no any interest in "holding" humans with his strong jaws. He will, however, grip a toy with unshakable enthusiasm, and one of his greatest delights is to pull with you in a cheerful tug of war.

Until he is trained, your Boxer will also have an instinctive desire to pull on his leash; he could easily drag you down the street. It is obvious that he must be firmly instructed in "civilized" behavior. He is not a dog for the proverbial "little old lady"—until he has learned his manners.

While I have called your attention to the Boxer's physical strength, it must be said that all his clownish and rough-and-tumble ways are usually tempered with good judgment. While he may gallop right at you as if to mow you down, he will (usually) turn aside at the last delicious moment.

The Ideal Boxer

All pedigreed dogs are bred to a particular standard, a kind of blueprint for the breed (for more, see the box on page 14). The most recent revision of the official breed standard of the Boxer was adopted by the American Kennel Club (AKC) in March 2005.

While you may never seek the near perfection of a great show dog, anyone seeking a Boxer as a pet must be mindful that the standard was also written to ensure soundness and good temperament—paramount qualities in any dog who lives in your household. It's important to familiarize yourself with the basic concept of the breed standard, so you can enjoy a healthy and happy, well-adjusted Boxer for many years.

General Appearance

According to the standard, the ideal Boxer combines strength and agility with elegance and style. His movements should suggest a dog of great energy—the stride free and the carriage proud.

The Boxer should be square when you consider the length of his body and the height of his legs. He has strong legs and well-developed muscles that appear smooth under taut skin.

Despite a current fashion to breed taller Boxers, the standard tells us that the Boxer "is a medium-sized, square built dog of good substance," and defines "medium-sized" as: "Adult males—23 to 25 inches; females—21½ to 23½ inches at the withers [the top of the shoulders]. Preferably, males should not be under the minimum nor females over the maximum." A taller dog who is to remain square will, of course, have a longer body to go with his greater height. The overall impression, then, is of a noticeably bigger, heavier animal than is called for in the standard. Breeders are often cautioned by judges and their peers not to go to extremes of size.

That Regal Head

The standard says, "The chiseled head imparts to the Boxer a unique individual stamp." The essence of breed type in the Boxer is embodied in his head—from the bone structure to the mood-mirroring quality of his eyes to his lips and chin. The head is what sets him apart from other breeds, and those who know him think of it as beautiful. To the uninitiated, the Boxer head may appear bizarre, but it was developed to enable him to do the job humans required of him. He had to be able to catch and hold fierce game—bear and wild boar—until the hunter caught up. While his jaws had to have great strength, he also had to be able to breathe with his mouth embedded in thick folds of hide and fur. These requirements were satisfied by his head's unique structure.

The standard says, "In judging the Boxer first consideration is given to general appearance and overall balance. Special attention is then devoted to the head." The head must be in correct proportion to the body, which means it should never be too large or too small.

The elegant, chiseled head, set atop a graceful neck, sets the Boxer apart.

What Is a Breed Standard?

A breed standard is a detailed description of the perfect dog of that breed. Breeders use the standard as a guide in their breeding programs, and judges use it to evaluate the dogs in conformation shows. The standard is written by the national breed club, using guidelines established by the registry that recognizes the breed (such as the AKC or UKC).

The first section of the breed standard gives a brief overview of the breed's history. Then it describes the dog's general appearance and size as an adult. Next is a detailed description of the head and neck, then the back and body, and the front and rear legs. The standard then describes the ideal coat and how the dog should be presented in the show ring. It also lists all acceptable colors, patterns, and markings. Then there's a section on how the dog moves, called *gait*. Finally, there's a general description of the dog's temperament.

Each section also lists characteristics that are considered to be faults or disqualifications in the conformation ring. Superficial faults in appearance are often what distinguish a pet-quality dog from a show- or competition-quality dog. However, some faults affect the way a dog moves or his overall health. And faults in temperament are serious business.

You can read all the AKC breed standards at www.akc.org.

The Muzzle

"The beauty of the head depends on the harmonious proportion of muzzle to skull," according to the standard. The muzzle should be two-thirds the width of the skull and one-third the length of the head from the occiput to the tip of the nose. (The occiput is the slightly rounded bony protuberance between the ears.) Skin wrinkles appear on the forehead and contribute to the Boxer's unique, slightly quizzical expression. They are desirable but should not be excessive (referred to as "wet").

The Eyes Have It

The Boxer's generous, full eyes are a dark brown color—the deeper shades are preferred. They must not be yellowish (known as "bird of prey" eyes). They should not be too round, slanted, or owlish, or too small. They reflect the dog's moods to an extraordinary degree, and you will soon learn to read them, to your advantage. In combination, the Boxer's eyes and wrinkles on his forehead create an expression—a sweet and gentle look—that is uniquely his.

All Ears

In the United States, the Boxer's ears are customarily cropped—surgically trimmed and shaped to make them stand upright. However, as the 2005 breed standard makes clear, cropping is strictly optional. (Ear cropping is prohibited in Great Britain and is discouraged in other parts of Europe.) When ears are cropped, this procedure is most commonly performed when the puppy is between 6 and 12 weeks old.

The Boxer was originally bred to catch and hold game—sometimes wild boar and other sizable prey—so historically, it was not desirable for him to have long, flapping, easily wounded ears. What began as a purely utilitarian practice ultimately became the fashion. However, many pet owners choose to keep the ears uncropped. In that case, they should lie flat to the cheeks. To crop or not to crop is purely a matter of individual preference.

The Skull

The Boxer's skull is slightly arched on top, not too flat or too rounded. The standard says, "The forehead shows a slight indentation between the eyes and forms a distinct stop with the topline of the muzzle." (The stop is the area where the muzzle meets the face.) One of the most important features of the Boxer's head is that the "tip of the nose should lie slightly higher than the root of the muzzle." In other words, the nose should tip up slightly. Historically, this is essential in a correct head so that the dog can breathe while holding his prey. This "tip-up" is very visible in profile.

The muzzle protrudes slightly in front of the nose, further ensuring the ability to breathe. The shape of the muzzle is influenced by the "formation of both jaw-bones through the placement of the teeth and through the texture of the lips."

Those Jaws

The Boxer is undershot; that is, the lower jaw protrudes beyond the upper jaw "and curves slightly upward," ideally with "the corner upper incisors fitting snugly back of the lower canine teeth," giving the Boxer an almost unshakable grip. "The

The Boxer is undershot, which means the lower jaw protrudes beyond the upper jaw.

front surface of the muzzle is broad and squarish." The canine teeth beneath the full lips contribute greatly to this look. They should be wide apart in both upper and lower jaws. The row of lower incisors should be straight, while the upper incisors should be slightly convex.

The distance between the upper and lower jaws should be definitive but not so pronounced as to ever show teeth or tongue when the mouth is closed. A wry mouth—where upper and lower jaws are slightly askew and out of line with each other—is a serious fault.

The lips should meet evenly in front. The upper lip does *not* lie over the lower lip. The lips are padded and thick, and the upper lip is supported by the canine teeth of the lower jaw beneath. The Boxer's chin must be prominent and visible both from the front and in profile.

The Body Beautiful

A natural athlete, the Boxer is designed for speed and endurance when required, reflecting his origins as a hunter, as well as his modern roles of guard and companion dog. While an elegant appearance, especially in the show ring, is attractive and often desirable, he must never be *weedy*. (A weedy dog has a small or light frame.) The dog must always give an impression of real substance—the natural consequence of strong bones and superbly conditioned muscles.

When we say that the Boxer is a square dog, we mean that a vertical line drawn from the highest point of the withers to the ground should equal a horizontal line drawn from the foremost projection of the chest (the sternum) to the rear projection of the upper thigh. To achieve squareness, the Boxer cannot be long through the loin or the back. If he is, he will inevitably look long, and the square, balanced appearance that is an essential feature of the breed will be lost.

The Tale of the Tail

The tail is set high on the back and is carried upward. Customarily it is docked, and anyone who has witnessed the furiously wagging tail of a happy Boxer will see the wisdom of docking. Not only would the long tail be a menace to furniture and toddlers, but it would also be subject to injury and trauma. Docking is done when puppies are only a few days old. At the same time, front dewclaws (vestigial claws a few inches above the paw) are removed to prevent their snagging and tearing later in life.

Color Choices

The standard says acceptable colors for a Boxer are fawn (shades of tan all the way to mahogany) and brindle (clearly defined black stripes on a fawn background). Brindling may be sparse, with only a few stripes, to exceedingly heavy, where the fawn background barely shows at all. This is known as "reverse" brindling. Both are equally acceptable. Whatever the coat color, Boxers should have a black mask on the face.

The coat is often enhanced by attractive white markings, which must not exceed one-third of the entire coat. In other words, if you can imagine the dog laid out like a bearskin rug, the white markings, including those on the stomach, must not exceed one-third of the body area.

Typically, white markings are found on the face in the form of a blaze and/or a portion of white on the muzzle. If the dog has white markings on the face, they will replace a part of the black mask. The dog may also have varying amounts of white on his front and rear legs, and a white chest and throat. However, white markings are not required under the breed standard.

Totally white or almost totally white Boxers are not uncommon in a litter of puppies. This is a disqualification under the breed standard. While they are not

All-white Boxers are not rare. It's only aesthetics that keeps them out of the show ring; they make great pets and can compete in canine sports.

eligible to compete in the show ring, they can be exhibited in obedience trials, agility, and other performance events. White Boxers make the same delightful pets as their fawn and brindle siblings.

All-Important Character

The character and temperament of the Boxer make him unique among dogs. The Boxer standard says that character and temperament "are of paramount importance." He is "instinctively a hearing guard dog." This means that he is always alert to strange noises or unusual occurrences that he might perceive as a threat to either himself or his family.

The standard continues, "[H]is bearing is alert, dignified, and self-assured. In the show ring his behavior should exhibit constrained animation. With family and friends, his temperament is fundamentally playful, yet patient and stoical with children. Deliberate and wary with strangers, he will exhibit curiosity, but, most importantly, fearless courage if threatened. However, he responds promptly to friendly overtures honestly rendered. His intelligence, loyal affection, and tractability to discipline make him a highly desirable companion."

A Boxer should be fearless, ready to defend and protect. Above all, however, a Boxer loves people—especially children. He is a boisterous, happy dog, always ready for a game or a romp in the woods. He responds with delight to "friendly overtures honestly rendered." No longer a hunter of boar or bear, he is happiest with the family that he will love beyond measure.

Boxers love people—especially children.

Chapter 2

Boxer History

The Boxer as we know the breed today is a product of selective breeding for many generations. Although her ancestors hark back to heavily built, short muzzled, fearless dogs bred in Assyria as early as 2500 BCE, the modern Boxer was largely developed in Germany in the late nineteenth and early twentieth centuries.

After the Franco-Prussian War of 1870 to 1871, Germany entered a period of relative calm and social stability. A citizenry that had been fighting just to survive at last had some leisure time, and in the 1870s and 1880s turned to refining a number of dog breeds. It was during this period that the Doberman Pinscher, Giant Schnauzer, and Great Dane came of age. The Boxer was developed from stocky Bullenbeissers, who were used to run down, catch, and hold fierce wild boar, bear, and bison. In the Middle Ages, they were Germany's only hunting hounds.

The Bullenbeisser had a wide, short muzzle that distinguished her from all other breeds of dog—then and now. She knew instinctively how to tackle the game from behind and hold it in a way that kept the dog from getting hurt, yet gave the hunters time to catch up and kill the game. These dogs were therefore highly prized and painstakingly bred.

However, after the Napoleonic Wars (1803–1815), many of Germany's ducal estates disbanded, and hunting became a less popular pursuit among the gentry. The last recorded boar hunt was held in 1865, after which the hunting dogs were sold. The Bullenbeissers' instincts made them useful dogs for butchers and cattle dealers, and many found homes with such merchants and traders. They also found favor with circus performers because of their native intelligence and ability to learn tricks.

Establishing the Boxer

As hunting was declining in popularity, the British exported to Germany a particular breed that they called a Bulldog but that actually resembled a small Mastiff. This dog was square and had long legs. Seventy years later, some of the pioneering Boxer breeders used two of these Bulldogs, Trutzel and Tom, to establish their lines. Tom sired the white female Ch. Blanka v. Angertor, and she was the dam of Meta von der Passage, whelped in 1898, a particolor (white with colored patches) who is the ancestor of almost all Boxers everywhere.

In 1895, the first Boxer club, called the Deutscher Boxer Club, was formed in Munich. Other German Boxer clubs followed. The first German breed standard was written and adopted in 1902. In 1905, all the German clubs combined. The early German breeders kept detailed records so we can clearly see the ancestry of the modern Boxer from about 1890 on.

Bull Baiting

In the early to mid-nineteenth century in Britain, dogs resembling modern Boxers with long tails were used to participate in the vicious "sport" of baiting bulls. These "baits" were held in roped-off enclosures, and the object was to see whether the dog could sneak under the horns of a tethered bull, grab him by his tender nose, and pin him to the ground. The bull would attempt to dislodge the dog by any means possible; terrible injuries to dog and bull resulted. Spectators lost and won large sums based on the outcome of such contests. Many lithographs, notably the work of Henry Alken in Britain, depict these cruel encounters. It was thought that the frantic struggles of the bull would tenderize his meat when he was eventually butchered.

The vom Dom Boxers

The development and refinement of the Boxer must be credited to the Germans—until the 1940s, when American breeders became involved in a meaningful way. In Germany, many breeders contributed to the breed in those early days, but in America no one has had as great an influence as the famous vom Dom kennels of Philip and Friederun Stockmann. The first vom Dom Boxer was registered in Germany in 1911. From modest beginnings, and with considerable difficulty during both World Wars, Friederun Stockmann bred some of the finest Boxers the world had yet seen. Her devotion to her dogs was legendary, and she worked tirelessly to keep them well cared for in an increasingly politically unstable Germany.

This 1823 lithograph by Henry Alken shows dogs who look a lot like Boxers being used for bull baiting.

Both Philip Stockmann and ten of the vom Dom dogs were sent to the front lines when World War I broke out. These dogs were used to guard prisoners and as sentries. In addition, they would sometimes be sent out to catch and bring down an enemy soldier—actions harking back to their earlier hunting days.

The first vom Dom connection to the United States was made in 1914, when Philip Stockmann returned from a show in Hamburg and announced to his wife that he had sold Dampf vom Dom after the dog had been awarded the Sieger (championship) title. At only 18 months of age, Dampf was exported to America, to the governor of New York, Herbert H. Lehman.

Unfortunately, because there were so few Boxer bitches in this country at the time, Dampf was not often used as a stud dog. Still, he left his mark on history. The first Boxer to be registered in the United States by the AKC was Arnulf Grandenz, recorded in 1904. But in 1915, Dampf became the first American Boxer champion.

Ivein vom Dom was whelped in January 1925, when Germany was slowly rebuilding after World War I. Although Ivein was not a champion, Friederun Stockmann sensed something special in the big fawn dog and kept him for breeding. He fathered the great German sire Sigurd vom Dom. During the five years he lived in Germany, Sigurd became known as an exceptional show dog and sire. He was said to exemplify the ideal balance of power and elegance. At the age of 5 he was sold to the Barmere Kennels in Van Nuys, California.

A Gentleman Amongst Dogs

In her book, *My Life With Boxers*, Friederun Stockmann writes, "The Boxer . . . is a gentleman amongst dogs with short coats. He not only wants the best food, he wants to be handled in a civilized manner too. He can easily be upset by his master and this is called being leader-sensitive. He cannot stand a hard hand or injustice. It is true that he is pigheaded and every one has a personality of its own. His real job is to be a house and family dog and to be a friend to the children."

Three of the greatest dogs the vom Dom kennels produced ended up in America—Sigurd, and his grandsons, Lustig and Utz. Lustig vom Dom was exported in 1937 and became Ch. Lustig v. Dom of Tulgey Wood. Lustig was sold only because a great price was offered for him at a time when the Stockmann family had very little money. Friederun Stockmann never saw Lustig again, but Philip did when he judged the Westminster Kennel Club show in 1938. Utz, three years younger than Lustig, arrived in the United States in 1939.

This photo shows Sigurd in Germany at a young age. He was considered an exceptional dog on both sides of the Atlantic.

The American Boxer

It is generally agreed that the modern Boxer in America owes her existence to four great foundation sires, all imported from Germany in the 1930s. They are:

- Sigurd vom Dom of Barmere, a fawn dog imported by Charles Ludwig for Miriam Breed (Barmere Kennels) in 1934 (Sigurd was the grandfather of the next three).
- Dorian vom Marienhof of Mazelaine, a brindle dog imported in 1935 by John and Mazie Wagner (Mazelaine Kennels); his sire was Int. Ch. Xerxes vom Dom, a full brother to the sire of Lustig and Utz.
- Lustig vom Dom of Tulgey Wood, a fawn dog imported in 1937 by Erwin Freund.
- Utz vom Dom of Mazelaine, a fawn dog imported by John and Mazie Wagner in 1939 (Utz and Lustig were full brothers).

There was already a small but dedicated contingent of Boxer enthusiasts in America in the early years of the twentieth century, and the American Boxer Club (ABC), the breed's U.S. parent club, was founded in 1935. The first ABC meeting was on February 16, 1935, in New York City. Mrs. Rudolph Gaertner, secretary, made a formal application for membership in the American Kennel Club on March 21. The club had seventeen members. AKC membership was granted in May 1935.

One of the first things the members did was ask the AKC to move Boxers from the Non-Sporting to the Working Group, and the Boxer became an official member of the Working Group on September 1, 1935. Some fanciers felt that the Boxer could not compete successfully against the popular Doberman Pinscher or Collie, and were disappointed. (Today Collies are part of the Herding Group, but that group was established by the AKC in 1983.) In time, however, Boxers were more than able to hold their own.

In 1938, Philip Stockmann was invited to judge the ABC specialty show. He awarded Best of Breed to the legendary Lustig. Stockmann

> ### The Great Lustig
>
> Lustig vom Dom sired forty-one champions for Erwin Freund's Tulgey Wood Kennels of Illinois. He came to the U.S. wearing a collar with the inscription, "I am the magnificent Lustig." Years later, Friederun Stockmann visited his grave at Tulgey Wood.

TIP

For more information about Boxer clubs, visit www.americanboxerclub. org/us-boxer-clubs.html.

attended the ABC annual meeting that week and was instrumental in creating the breed standard. White markings, not always welcome in the early days of the breed, were to be permitted. However, he suggested that Boxers who were more than one-third white be disqualified. Although by that time at least one had finished his U.S. championship, the ABC adopted the disqualification. It stands today.

Ch. Bang Away of Sirrah Crest

On February 17, 1949, a flashy fawn puppy bred and owned by Dr. and Mrs. R.C. Harris was whelped at their Sirrah Crest Kennels in California. He was a direct descendant of Dorian vom Marienhof. He grew up to be the incomparable Ch. Bang Away of Sirrah Crest, winner of 121 all-breed Bests in Show and sire of eighty-one U.S. champions. No other Boxer whelped before or since has come close to approximating his stunning record as a show dog or a producer. He left behind seven American Boxer Club–designated Sires and Dams of Merit. (To be a Sire or Dam of Merit, a sire must produce at least seven champions, a dam must produce at least four, and the rare Legion of Merit producer must have sired or given birth to four Sires and/or Dams of Merit).

the **DOG NEWS**

THE BOXER
DORIAN v. MARIENHOF OF MAZELAINE
Owned by Dr. and Mrs. John P. Wagner, Mazelaine Kennels, Milwaukee, Wisc.

"The National Dog Magazine"

May, 1936   20c Per Copy

The year after Dorian arrived in the United States, he was already a cover dog.

Bang Away's showmanship was legendary, and it was evidenced very early—at only 10 weeks of age he was chosen Best in Match out of ninety puppies judged by Friederun Stockmann herself, who was visiting in California. She referred to him as "Little Lustig."

In 1951, Bang Away achieved the great distinction of being Best in Show at the Westminster Kennel Club dog show in New York City. He was the third Boxer to take that honor. (The other two were Ch. Warlord of Mazelaine in 1947 and Ch. Mazelaine's Zazarac Brandy in 1949.) The next Boxer to win

What Is the AKC?

The American Kennel Club (AKC) is the oldest and largest pure-bred dog registry in the United States. Its main function is to record the pedigrees of dogs of the breeds it recognizes. While AKC registration papers are a guarantee that a dog is pure-bred, they are absolutely not a guarantee of the quality of the dog—as the AKC itself will tell you.

The AKC makes the rules for all the canine sporting events it sanctions and approves judges for those events. It is also involved in various public education programs and legislative efforts regarding dog ownership. More recently, the AKC has helped establish a foundation to study canine health issues and a program to register microchip numbers for companion animal owners. The AKC has no individual members—its members are national and local breed clubs and clubs dedicated to various competitive sports.

Westminster would have to wait almost twenty years: Ch. Arriba's Prima Donna in 1970.

Bang Away was a flashy Boxer, meaning he had a striking amount of white on his face and feet. Until his day, Boxers in America tended to be plainer—marked with less white. The love affair with flash continues into the twenty-first century, although in recent years the ABC has made it clear that white markings are not necessary according to the breed standard.

Rising Popularity

The popularity of the Boxer in America surged in the 1950s. It seemed as though everywhere you looked, someone was walking a Boxer down the street. Press coverage of the three Westminster wins, plus the Boxer's natural virtues of medium size and a short and tidy coat, contributed to her popularity. Celebrities were quick to fall in love with the breed. In addition, it was becoming well publicized that while she remained an excellent guard and watchdog, she was

Famous Boxer Owners

Lauren Bacall
Humphrey Bogart
Nat King Cole
Broderick Crawford
J. Edgar Hoover
Ice-T
Luke Perry
Elvis Presley
Babe Ruth
Sylvester Stallone
Shirley Temple
Justin Timberlake

extremely fond of children and a friend to almost all who approached her with good intentions. The Boxer was ranked number two in AKC breed registrations in 1955 and 1956.

Of course, all this attention rarely does a breed any lasting good, and the Boxer fell victim to less scrupulous breeders who were out to make a fast dollar. Both health and temperament suffered as a result. However, those dedicated breeders who truly loved and admired the Boxer kept patiently breeding quality animals. It did not take long for the Boxer to rebound with her usual good humor and the many fine qualities for which she is known.

Today's Boxer

In the 1960s and early 1970s, breeders continued to develop and refine the Boxer. Their work has contributed to the taller, more elegant animal we know today. Not everyone agreed with the trends, but they are facts, nonetheless.

In the 1980s and 1990s, the Boxer had settled into comfortable AKC registration figures. From 1991 through 1993 she ranked seventeenth. In 2007 she ranked sixth in registrations among all AKC breeds—a rise in popularity that concerns conscientious breeders, who do not wish to see the breed exploited or bred carelessly.

Today, the American Boxer Club has about 900 members all over the United States and Canada. ABC members are dedicated to the welfare of the breed worldwide. There are about 60 ABC member clubs, spread across almost every state, and Boxer lovers are encouraged to join these clubs at the local level—great places to be educated. Ultimately, regional club members may seek ABC membership.

The Boxer has become a successful guide dog for the visually impaired, a certified specialist trained to help the physically handicapped, and a well-mannered visitor bringing cheer to nursing homes. Increasingly, the Boxer has been used in police work and search and rescue activities. In fact, Boxers figured prominently in recovery work in the aftermath of the terrorist attack on September 11, 2001.

Chapter 3

Why Choose a Boxer?

A Boxer has a great sense of humor. His antics around the house are a constant source of amusement to his human guardians. A Boxer is one of the few dogs who enjoys playing all by himself. If no human is available, he may pick up a toy or a tissue from the wastebasket (beware—wastebaskets are regarded as a Boxer's private stash!) and parade around the house, tossing his prize not-so-delicately in the air and rolling over on it on the rug. You may return from an afternoon's shopping and find that rug swept to one side on the floor, and a Boxer greeting you with an impish glint in his eyes. Or, as in the case of a friend of ours, you may find your shoes tossed down the stairs, a gesture clearly designed to tell you you've been absent too long!

A Boxer has an instinctive desire to be clean. He will groom himself constantly in a catlike fashion, licking off offending dirt and using his paws to wipe his face. This natural tendency is easily channeled into quick and easy housetraining for the young puppy—no self-respecting Boxer will have any part of soiling himself or his bed.

Contrary to popular myth, a Boxer does not drool any more than most dogs. In fact, the only time he will drool is if he is constantly rewarded by begging for food at the table. A Boxer does, however, accumulate water in his flews when drinking, and if he happens to shake his head soon after, onlookers beware!

As a breed, Boxers definitely are not natural water dogs. Most Boxers hate to immerse even their tiniest toe in extraneous water droplets. If it's raining and it is time for your Boxer to answer a call of nature, he will look at you in amazement at the mere *suggestion* that he should venture outside. One of our friends owned a female Boxer who, when absolutely required to relieve herself in

> **Boxer Characteristics**
>
> Sensitive
> Intelligent
> Courageous
> Athletic
> Easily bored
> Loves children
> Jealous of your affections
> Playful
> Clean
> Sometimes aggressive with other dogs

inclement weather, would go to the door and turn delicately around. With her front paws still on the threshold, she would do her duty and rush back inside. Before we realized the Boxer's aversion to water, my husband threw a stick into a small pond on our property. Our 7-month-old puppy leapt gaily after it, only to surface in abject astonishment and disgust. Though swimming came naturally to her, she never went into the pond again in all her long life.

Resourceful Intelligence

Those of us who are fortunate enough to live with a Boxer(s) can cite many instances that illustrate his innate ability to reason. I'm thinking of a puppy named Bo who, when placed in a crate for the first time, watched with great interest while I securely fastened the latch, then calmly reached out and carefully *lifted* the latch and calmly walked free. And did it again. And again.

I'm thinking of a dog named Dylan who departed for a week of dog shows without his beloved green rubber frog. When he returned home at last, he raced through the house, up the stairs, and behind the distant door where he knew he had left his cherished prize.

I'm thinking of a dog named Gus who rode across Long Island Sound on the auto ferry with me on one bright summer afternoon. It was a pleasurable trip (Gus's first), replete with lots of Fritos and oatmeal cookies offered by the kids who decided Gus was fascinating. When the trip ended, we found ourselves in

> **A True Homebody**
>
> While the Boxer is an exciting show dog, he is always happiest at home with those he loves. Indeed it is his loyalty and sweet disposition that have endeared him to his legions of admirers over the years.

the middle of a long line of disembarking passengers impatiently threading their way among the tightly spaced cars on the auto deck. Suddenly, disaster loomed. The tiny spaces had grown so small that no seventy-five-pound male Boxer could physically maneuver another step. Harried passengers glared at us without pity. We could not proceed;

Boxers are amazingly intelligent. This makes them extremely interesting but not so easy to train.

we could not retreat. The line halted. I nervously looked down at Gus, who was anxiously looking up at me, and I said something very close to the following, aloud: "Gus, there is no way we can do this unless you get down on your belly and crawl underneath these cars so we can get out of here."

My big, sweet, full-of-cookies dog gazed right into my eyes, lowered his body, and crawled under three cars while I struggled to keep up. The man in front of me gasped at this prodigious intellectual feat; the pink-hatted lady behind me shook her head in disbelief; I myself was mightily impressed. Gus was justifiably proud of himself and jauntily completed his navigation of the auto maze without further complication. Obedience at short notice was his specialty.

Training Challenges

That said, training your Boxer can be a challenge. You will find that he is of superior canine intelligence. This intellect, combined with his independence, demands a strong trainer, one who is wise in the ways of such dogs. First, we must remember that a Boxer gets bored very easily. While he can be quickly taught everything from polite behavior to parlor tricks, he will not perform reliably if he sees no point to the exercise.

Therefore, teaching a Boxer must be made fun for the dog. He must look forward to these sessions, not dread them. Boredom may be mistaken for stubbornness. Most (not all) trainers use edible treats and much praise to enhance these exercises. Gradually, as the dog consistently obeys, praise replaces the goodies. And in time, certain learned behaviors, such as walking on a loose leash, simply become second nature to the dog.

No Boxer owner will ever attempt to equate "obedience" with "intelligence." A Boxer basically does what he does when he feels like doing it—but he learns like lightning. A Boxer needs to know *why* he should do something, *why* he should interrupt his leisure to pursue some silly human desire. If you give him reason enough, the Boxer just may perform for you—and do it in style. But a Boxer without a reason is a Boxer immovable.

Boxers Love Kids

A Boxer is apt to be gentler and less bold with women than with men, and when he meets children, magic happens. Boxers adore children. If you walk a Boxer down a crowded street, you will invariably find that his attention is engaged by kids of all shapes and sizes. He finds them fascinating creatures, and in your household he will almost always be found beside the littlest people around. Your Boxer will take any amount of abuse from a child without a thought of retaliation. Indeed, he will seem to thrive on the sometimes careless games a child may invent for his dog—the 2-year-old's "Let's pour sand on him" or "Let's pull his tail" game, or the 7-year-old's "Let's dress Rover up in mom's clothes" antics.

Boxers seem to understand instinctively the physical limitations of kids—from tiny tots to teens. Babies are regarded with the utmost respect, and you may often find your Boxer parked soulfully next to a crib, gently contemplating the infant therein.

Boxers are very protective of children, and many a mother has left her toddler briefly in a Boxer's care while her back was turned, secure in the knowledge that no harm would come to the baby if the dog was nearby. Indeed, your Boxer will have a special regard for all humans he understands to be helpless or handicapped—not only kids, but also the sick and infirm.

Children adore Boxers—and the feeling is mutual.

The Dog's Senses

The dog's eyes are designed so that he can see well in relative darkness, has excellent peripheral vision, and is very good at tracking moving objects—all skills that are important to a carnivore. Dogs also have good depth perception. Those advantages come at a price, though: Dogs are nearsighted and are slow to change the focus of their vision. It's a myth that dogs are color-blind. However, while they can see some (but not all) colors, their eyes were designed to most clearly perceive subtle shades of gray—an advantage when they are hunting in low light.

Dogs have about six times fewer taste buds on their tongue than humans do. They can taste sweet, sour, bitter, and salty tastes, but with so few taste buds it's likely that their sense of taste is not very refined.

A dog's ears can swivel independently, like radar dishes, to pick up sounds and pinpoint their location. Dogs can locate a sound in $6/100$ of a second and hear sound four times farther away than we can (which is why there is no reason to yell at your dog). They can also hear sounds at far higher pitches than we can.

In their first few days of life, puppies primarily use their sense of touch to navigate their world. Whiskers on the face, above the eyes, and below the jaws are sensitive enough to detect changes in airflow. Dogs also have touch-sensitive nerve endings all over their bodies, including on their paws.

Smell may be a dog's most remarkable sense. Dogs have about 220 million scent receptors in their nose, compared to about 5 million in humans, and a large part of the canine brain is devoted to interpreting scent. Not only can dogs smell scents that are very faint, but they can also accurately distinguish between those scents. In other words, when you smell a pot of spaghetti sauce cooking, your dog probably smells tomatoes and onions and garlic and oregano and whatever else is in the pot.

The Green-Eyed Monster

A Boxer is a jealous dog. He is insistent and demanding of your affection, and thus, he is jealous of every living creature who could come between him and his family members. If one Boxer tries to curl up on your lap (an interesting feat!), you will have two Boxers vying for the same space; if the family cat gets a pat on the head, the Boxer will insist on his due. He is also jealous and possessive about objects such as toys and food dishes. If a dozen rubber "squeakies" are scattered about the rug, you can count on two Boxers coveting the same latex mouse. Likewise, food dishes are zealously guarded.

Boxers, as a rule, are not inordinately fond of other dogs. They would really much prefer not having to share their world with other canines who might at any time occupy your attention. Sometimes, this lack of sociability and jealousy can take a very serious turn. Boxers have been implicated in dogfights, with grave consequences. Usually, two Boxers of opposite sexes will live happily together; trouble is more likely to erupt if two males share the same household. There may be equal nastiness if two bitches decide not to get along.

Once a Boxer takes a dislike to another dog, regardless of breed, it is very difficult, if not impossible, to change his mind. Pacifism is not a breed characteristic. Sometimes, if you are lucky, your Boxers will quietly establish a pecking order in the

Two Boxers of opposite sexes will usually live together peacefully, but two of the same sex is asking for trouble.

household. Without obvious signs, one dog will dominate, and the others will accept his or her leadership.

Years ago we lived with three adult male Boxers in the family—a sire and two sons. These dogs were inseparable: They slept in a sloppy pile together; they ate side by side; there was never a glimmer of trouble. In the course of time, the older dog died. Within two weeks, the two brothers—the same two brothers who spent all their time playing in perfect harmony—would have quite literally fought to the death.

Boxers are alert dogs, but they're not noisy.

No amount of psychology ever changed the situation, and they lived behind closed doors for the rest of their lives.

This situation is not an unusual one. In this particular case, it seems clear that the sire exerted dominance over the sons, and they accepted it. After his death, however, the younger animals vied for superiority, and each refused to yield. While situations like this are not unique to the Boxer breed, you must remember that they are powerful animals and they cannot be taken for granted.

Listen to the Silence

One of the Boxer's great virtues is his relative silence. If you attend a Boxer national specialty (a dog show with only Boxers), you will be struck by the lack of canine noise you hear. That is not to say your Boxer has no voice. Rather, he has a loud, booming, almost roaring bark when he feels the need to warn. He simply uses his vocal capabilities sparingly and only after thinking the situation over. Known as a hearing guard dog, he will generally bark when a stranger enters his yard or another dog dares to cross his boundary line. Thus, he is a very effective watchdog. If the stranger is invited in, he will most likely become your Boxer's best friend—but we try not to publicize that fact!

I have only just touched on the essence of the Boxer. They are at once fun, frustrating, lovable, obstinate, uncannily bright, and great clowns. They will make your home a happier place. When we lose them, as we inevitably must, we shall remember the morning they stole a pound of butter from the kitchen; we shall remember the tails that wagged with delight every time they saw us; we shall remember their sweetly quizzical expressions and their unquestioning love.

Chapter 4

Choosing
Your Boxer

A Boxer puppy will bring you untold joy—and she will try your patience. She will interrupt your sleep and wreak havoc with your daily routine. She will walk through her water bowl and spit up on the rug. But she will also snuggle up beside you, lick your face, and tell you in all her extensive Boxer vocabulary that you are the greatest human on earth. She will help make life worth living.

Finding a Reputable Breeder

The best place to buy a Boxer is from a reputable breeder. Good breeders usually have a track record of producing healthy, well-adjusted pups over a period of years. While they may breed to show in conformation or performance events, they sell many more pups than they will ever keep. And you, the buyer, reap the reward of all those years of careful selection for soundness and temperament.

You can find good private breeders by contacting your local kennel club. (Try www.akc.org for referrals through the AKC.) If there is a local dog show, that's also a great place to make contact with fine breeders. Perhaps a friend or neighbor has a Boxer you admire—they may be an excellent referral for you.

A reputable breeder will allow you to come to his home (by appointment, please!), and perhaps see the sire and/or dam of the litter. You can make judgments based on the cleanliness of his facilities, the care with which he has raised his pups, and the temperament you observe in his dogs.

Research the Breeder!

After the breeder asks you all his questions, you should have your own list.

How many years has he been breeding Boxers?

If he exhibits in conformation or performance events, have his dogs won titles? (While numbers of titles are less important, it is a good idea to achieve some, to prove that his breeding program is successful.)

Are his facilities clean?

Are his adult dogs well groomed and happy?

Has the breeder done necessary health checks on the sire and dam? (For more information, see chapter 8.)

Is the breeder willing to provide any health guarantees for your pup? If so, do they seem reasonable? (Remember, no breeder can realistically guarantee disease-free life; nature is not perfect.)

Will the breeder supply you with AKC registration papers; medical, vaccination, and worming records; and the dog's pedigree?

Does the breeder appear to be willing to help and advise you?

Will the breeder help you with ear taping if the puppy's ears are cropped?

Is the pup being sold on a spay or neuter contract? (If so, this should be provided at time of sale.)

The breeder will ask you a lot of questions, and that's perfectly normal. He wants to make sure his dogs all end up in excellent homes. Do not be put off if your puppy's owner puts you through the "third degree," on the phone or via e-mail, asking questions like, "Where will the puppy sleep? Where will the puppy stay while you're at work? Do you have a fenced-in yard? If you owned a dog before, what happened to her?" All of these questions are designed

Reputable breeders start their puppies off right.

to determine whether yours is a suitable home for the sweet puppy the breeder has lovingly raised for her first weeks of life. Beware the person who does *not* ask you such questions.

You may be placed on a waiting list by the breeder—who usually does not have more than a litter or two per year, so he cannot supply a puppy at a moment's notice. This is usual and perfectly acceptable, although it might not always fit in with your schedule. If for some reason you are not able to wait for his expected litter, a good breeder may refer you to another breeder—networking within the world of responsible Boxer owners.

When you do make a purchase, the breeder will supply you with AKC registration papers, a pedigree, and a record of vaccinations and wormings to date. Hopefully, you will enjoy a long relationship with your Boxer's breeder—a valuable association for both you and the dog. All the years of experience your breeder has had will enable him to provide you with invaluable advice if any problems arise. And he will always stand behind you, ready to help if necessary, or re-home your Boxer if unforeseen circumstances require it.

Your Boxer may well be sold to you on a Limited AKC registration. This means your dog enjoys all the privileges attached to "full" registration, but must not be bred. Puppies from a dog with a Limited registration cannot be registered with the AKC. The breeder may have many reasons for this decision—for example, knowing that you do want to breed, or believing that your dog might not make a desirable contribution to the gene pool for whatever reason. In fact, it is not uncommon for a breeder to require a spay/neuter agreement at the time of sale. This requirement usually stipulates that your dog be neutered or spayed at or around the time of sexual maturity.

Backyard Breeders

Backyard breeders are usually people who have a pet dog and/or bitch and decide either to make some money by selling puppies, or want to have a litter to show their children the "miracle of birth." Often they are well meaning, and sometimes these people will produce perfectly acceptable pets. However, they do not have experience with the breed and may not be breeding for soundness of body and mind. Their breeding pair may not have had thorough health testing and can have many faults of conformation and temperament.

Rescue Organizations

Unfortunately, not all Boxers find happy homes. They are sometimes victimized by ignorant or cruel owners, or find themselves homeless as a result of divorce or the death of a loving owner. If they're lucky, these dogs find their way to a Boxer rescue group. Those people who work to rescue such animals are usually selfless and totally dedicated to the welfare of their charges. Do not hesitate to adopt from such rescue groups, especially when the history of the Boxer is known.

> **T I P**
>
> Rescue organizations can be found by contacting the AKC or the American Boxer Club (see the appendix).

If a Boxer is given up to a shelter in your municipality, this is also a perfectly acceptable way to acquire your dog—and perform a rescue of your own. Remember, an adult dog long past the housetraining stage may be a great addition to your family. A puppy is adorable—but a puppy grows up fast and requires attention to training and discipline that an older dog may not need.

Picking Your Puppy

Choosing a puppy is usually a happy expedition to the breeder's home or kennel. Which puppy in the litter will be yours? The breeder may offer you a choice of only one or two. That's perfectly all right. There are very likely to be "reservations" for one or more of the babies—people who left deposits even before birth.

If you do have a choice, be sure to pick a lively, alert animal, one who bounces up to greet you and wants to interact with the family. Do not be taken by the shy, shivering pup in the corner, no matter how sorry you may feel for her. Remember, she was raised under the same conditions as her littermates and for reasons unknown to you has not developed into a happy, well-adjusted animal.

Knowing all these things well in advance of our first puppy purchase, my husband and I went one afternoon to see a litter of tumbling, bumbling 8-week-old Boxers. We had a choice of six. Wisely remembering the latest dog book he

Boy or girl? In fact, it doesn't make much difference.

had read, my husband dropped a ring of keys into the midst of the babies. Five puppies rushed to investigate—a very good temperament test. They were curious and not in the least shy. One pretty male pup eyed the keys, looked at us, and calmly picked up a piece of a blanket and walked under a chair to chew it. He ignored us in the extreme. Of course, we said, "We'll have that one!" He grew up to be American/ Canadian Ch. Gray Roy's Minstrel Boy, LOM (also known as Casey), and was an adored and well-adjusted family member for all his days.

A Boy or a Girl?

Many people, seeking a pet for the family, will ask me which gender they should get. Usually, they assume that the female of the species is quieter and gentler. While the female Boxer is certainly smaller in physical size, she is not necessarily a more gentle animal than her male counterpart. I have known females who were pure hellions and males who were calm and mellow. Gender does not determine your Boxer's nature, and the individual disposition of any given dog will determine his or her behavior.

Consider an Adult Dog

There is nothing quite like the day you bring an adorable puppy home to your family. Puppies can be trained from an early age, and mistakes made or successes achieved are *your* mistakes and successes. However, puppies require a lot of time, effort, and just plain work: cleaning up messes; perhaps taping ears; and running home several times a day during work hours to let the puppy relieve herself—all necessary infringements of your time.

An older dog is usually past these puppy stages and is just eager to love you because you are giving her a caring home. Often, she has experienced some sort of loss, adversity, or neglect, and will be especially happy to have a new home.

Puppies are cute, but adult dogs have their advantages.

Occasionally, a breeder has kept a puppy as a prospective show or performance dog, and for some reason has decided against this—usually due to minor faults of conformation. This may be an excellent opportunity for you to purchase a very young adult raised in optimal circumstances.

The adult Boxer who does not have any serious bad habits may just be the right choice for your family. It is strictly a matter of personal preference. You also might fall in love with an older dog who needs a comfortable bed and a place to be loved for her later years; she would be forever grateful for your kindness.

Part II

Caring for Your Boxer

Chapter 5

Bringing Your Boxer Home

Y ou have a lot to do before your new dog comes home. Imagine if you had a new human baby; your nursery would be ready when he came home from the hospital. So, too, must your puppy's new home be made ready for him.

Fencing Saves Lives

There is no phone call a breeder fears as much as the sobbing owner who says that her dear puppy has just been lost or hit by a car. While nothing can absolutely guarantee this will never happen, you will go a long way toward protecting your Boxer if you fence in his play area. You don't have to enclose the entire yard, just an area large enough for some modest exercise where the puppy can also relieve himself.

A Boxer can easily leap six-foot fencing, but five to six feet in height is usually quite enough to keep your dog at home. Boxers, with some notable exceptions, tend not to be escape artists. Nevertheless, vigilance on your part is warranted. Be sure the fencing is buried at least six inches into the ground to discourage digging underneath.

Chain link, stockade fencing (with the added advantage that the neighbor's dog cannot see inside), or even tall pickets will do the job nicely. So-called invisible fencing relies on an electric current that mildly shocks the dog if he is wearing a special collar and comes too close to a hidden boundary. Most Boxers learn these bounds very quickly. But remember that the invisible barriers will not keep other dogs or wild animals out—or people who mean your dog harm.

The Crate

I strongly urge you to buy a dog crate. They come in molded plastic or wire mesh, and you should choose a size large enough for an adult Boxer to comfortably stand up and lie down in and easily turn around. Wire crates are sometimes preferable for air circulation during warm summer months, while the more closed confines of a durable plastic crate are better for the winter. Remember, too, that whenever you ride in the car, your Boxer should be in a crate for his own safety—a similar concept to that of a child seat for your small child.

Crates for adults are in the range of twenty-one inches wide by thirty-six inches long. You will save money by buying the adult size for your puppy—he grows up quickly! If you buy a wire crate, be sure the mesh is not so widely spaced that your puppy can get his head through—puppies can insert their heads into very small spaces. The danger here is that he will not be able to extract himself and may panic and choke.

Now that I've issued that warning, let me tell you that a crate will make your life much easier. They are useful for two things: housetraining and your pup's physical safety. A Boxer is a naturally clean dog. He most definitely does not want to soil either himself or his bed. Therefore, if a puppy is secure in a closed crate while you are unavoidably away from home, he will try very hard to contain himself until he is released. Believe me, it works. Also, while you are away, he cannot chew on electrical cords or eat something toxic left in an unguarded place.

Your puppy will come to look on the crate as his own special place and may enter it at will if you leave the door open. It will become a safe haven for him even into his adult years, a place where he can rest and relax. Remember that it has its important uses, but he should never be locked away to spend the majority of his time gazing soulfully out at the family.

You'll definitely need a dog crate—and a leash for when your puppy is out of the crate.

Puppy Essentials

You'll need to go shopping *before* you bring your puppy home. There are many, many adorable and tempting items at pet supply stores, but these are the basics.

- **Food and water dishes.** Look for bowls that are wide and low or weighted in the bottom so they will be harder to tip over. Stainless steel bowls are a good choice because they are easy to clean (plastic never gets completely clean) and almost impossible to break. Avoid bowls that place the food and water side by side in one unit—it's too easy for your dog to get his water dirty that way.
- **Leash.** A six-foot leather leash will be easy on your hands and very strong.
- **Collar.** Start with a nylon buckle collar. For a perfect fit, you should be able to insert two fingers between the collar and your pup's neck. Your dog will need larger collars as he grows up.
- **Crate.** Choose a sturdy crate that is easy to clean and large enough for your puppy to stand up, turn around, and lie down in.
- **Nail cutters.** Get a good, sharp pair that are the appropriate size for the nails you will be cutting. Your dog's breeder or veterinarian can give you some guidance here.
- **Grooming tools.** Different kinds of dogs need different kinds of grooming tools. See chapter 7 for advice on what to buy.
- **Chew toys.** Dogs *must* chew, especially puppies. Make sure you get things that won't break or crumble off in little bits, which the dog can choke on. Very hard plastic bones are a good choice. Do not feed rawhide or other materials that can become impacted in your puppy's digestive tract.
- **Toys.** Watch for sharp edges and unsafe items such as plastic eyes that can be swallowed. Many toys come with squeakers, which dogs can also tear out and swallow. All dogs will eventually destroy their toys; as each toy is torn apart, replace it with a new one.

Collar and Leash

A collar and leash are important items to have on hand for the new arrival. Be sure the collar is a flat type made of soft leather or synthetic materials. There is no need for a "choke" or training collar at this time. (They are perfectly fine for the adult Boxer, and may afford you a bit more control—something to think about as you walk an active, strong adult dog.) Be sure the flat collar is adjustable as the puppy grows, and that you fasten it so that he cannot pull it over his head.

Personally, I never have a collar on either a puppy or an adult dog unless I am physically present and am planning to take the dog out for a walk. Remember that your Boxer is a physically active dog. Collars can get snagged on all kinds of things: tree limbs, cabinet doors, furniture, the crate. *No collar is absolutely safe. Therefore, take no chances.* However, a collar and a leash are very necessary to teach your puppy to walk calmly at your side.

The leash itself does not need to be more than six feet long and should be strong leather or nylon, with a quality fastener made of sturdy metal. If you want a longer lead, the retractable Flexi leads are excellent. You select them according to the weight and strength ratings appropriate to the growing puppy and eventual adult. As the puppy grows older, the longer Flexi lead will afford him some real exercise opportunity.

A Comfy Bed

Your Boxer will love a nice, soft bed. Whether he is a puppy or an adult, he likes his creature comforts. A synthetic fleece blanket in his crate, or a soft commercial dog bed available from pet supply stores, will make him very happy. Of course, he is happiest of all in *your* bed. Allowing him the luxury of your sheets is up to you—but do remember that the adorable ten-pound puppy is going to grow up to weigh many times that!

Be sure that your Boxer sleeps out of drafts; he does not have a heavy coat to keep him warm. This is especially important for the new puppy, who has, up until now, had the physical presence of his mother and littermates to keep him cozy. A hot water bottle wrapped up in an old blanket or towel will help him feel secure for his first days in his new home.

Toys, Toys, Toys!

Toys are important for puppies and adult dogs alike. Your Boxer revels in play, and toys are a central focus of his world. If you do not supply them, your Boxer will create his own toys—by raiding the trash bin, taking a magazine off a counter, or finding your socks under the bed.

The most important toy you can give your new puppy, and one he will never tire of as long as he lives, is a sturdy, synthetic, almost indestructible bone. These

Toys are not a luxury for dogs. They absolutely need things to chew on and play with. Choose your puppy's toys with safety in mind.

are usually made of tough, hard nylon. They come in various shapes and sizes. The packaging will inform you that they are impregnated with an attractive (to dogs!) odor, but your Boxer will chew on it long after any artificial odor has wafted away.

While your puppy is teething, especially between 4 and 6 months of age, a nylon bone is almost a necessity—it will save the furniture. Although a Boxer is not a notorious chewer by nature and usually grows out of the teething stage rather quickly, why take chances with Aunt Martha's antiques? Be sure *not* to buy rawhide in any form. Boxers do love it but tend to end up with masses of it impacted in their intestines, with dire medical consequences. Natural bone can splinter and cause internal damage. For the same reason, stay away from the popular "chew hooves" and pig's feet or ears.

Latex toys are lots of fun, especially those that contain squeakers. Eventually, your Boxer will extract and swallow the squeaker, so beware. He will also cheerfully dismantle the latex while you watch. We only allow latex toys for a short play period while we are supervising.

Soft flying discs that cannot splinter or, indeed, soft toys of any kind, are also great playthings. Just watch for signs of destruction so the dog does not end up swallowing parts of his toy. Boxers especially love these fabric toys—fleece is a great choice. One of the favorites at our house is a fuzzy lion whose whiskers seem especially delectable.

Balls are also of great appeal. Do be sure that they are soft enough that they cannot break your puppy's teeth, and be certain they are large enough that they cannot be swallowed in one great gulp or become stuck in the throat. Tennis balls are *too small!* Pet supply stores and some of the dog food/equipment chain stores offer many good choices.

Puppy-Proofing Inside and Out

A house or yard is a potentially dangerous place for a puppy. Remember how you put special childproof locks on doors while your toddler was growing up? A puppy needs the same security in his environment. Electrical outlets, for example, are potential hazards. Puppies left to their own devices love to chew on outlets and cords.

Curious puppies and inquisitive dogs get into trouble not because they are bad, but simply because they want to investigate the world around them. It's our job to protect our dogs from harmful substances.

Houseplants may look lovely on the windowsill, but are they lethal if swallowed? I well remember a Christmas season and a bouncy litter of 12-week-olds. While my back was turned "only for a minute," they managed to tumble a Jerusalem cherry plant from the kitchen counter. All ended well, but my vet's cheerful admonition to induce vomiting meant a very long and messy night!

In our modern world, fertilizers and chemicals are everywhere on our lawns and in our gardens. Many of these products are toxic to dogs— including cedar mulches, which are often treated with arsenic. It is so important that you do not let your puppy run loose with abandon—he can pick up toxins on his paws and may lick them and ingest dangerous chemicals. Likewise, many outdoor gardens contain attractive but poisonous plants. You must be sure that your puppy does not decide to munch on any of these.

All his life, you will need to keep your dog safe and secure behind a sturdy fence.

Puppy-Proofing Your Home

You can prevent much of the destruction puppies can cause and keep your new dog safe by looking at your home and yard from a dog's point of view. Get down on all fours and look around. Do you see loose electrical wires, cords dangling from the blinds, or chewy shoes on the floor? Your pup will see them, too!

In the kitchen:

- Put all knives and other utensils away in drawers.
- Get a trash can with a tight-fitting lid.
- Put all household cleaners in cupboards that close securely; consider using childproof latches on the cabinet doors.

In the bathroom:

- Keep all household cleaners, medicines, vitamins, shampoos, bath products, perfumes, makeup, nail polish remover, and other personal products in cupboards that close securely; consider using childproof latches on the cabinet doors.
- Get a trash can with a tight-fitting lid.
- Don't use toilet bowl cleaners that release chemicals into the bowl every time you flush.
- Keep the toilet bowl lid down.
- Throw away potpourri and any solid air fresheners.

In the bedroom:

- Securely put away all potentially dangerous items, including medicines and medicine containers, vitamins and supplements, perfumes, and makeup.
- Put all your jewelry, barrettes, and hairpins in secure boxes.
- Pick up all socks, shoes, and other chewables.

In the rest of the house:

- Tape up or cover electrical cords; consider childproof covers for unused outlets.
- Knot or tie up any dangling cords from curtains, blinds, and the telephone.
- Securely put away all potentially dangerous items, including medicines and medicine containers, vitamins and supplements, cigarettes, cigars, pipes, and pipe tobacco, pens, pencils, felt-tip markers, craft and sewing supplies, and laundry products.
- Put all houseplants out of reach.
- Move breakable items off low tables and shelves.
- Pick up all chewable items, including television and electronics remote controls, cell phones, shoes, socks, slippers and sandals, food, dishes, cups and utensils, toys, books and magazines, and anything else that can be chewed on.

In the garage:

- Store all gardening supplies and pool chemicals out of reach of the dog.
- Store all antifreeze, oil, and other car fluids securely, and clean up any spills by hosing them down for at least ten minutes.
- Put all dangerous substances on high shelves or in cupboards that close securely; consider using childproof latches on the cabinet doors.
- Pick up and put away all tools.
- Sweep the floor for nails and other small, sharp items.

In the yard:

- Put the gardening tools away after each use.
- Make sure the kids put away their toys when they're finished playing.
- Keep the pool covered or otherwise restrict your pup's access to it when you're not there to supervise.
- Secure the cords on backyard lights and other appliances.
- Inspect your fence thoroughly. If there are any gaps or holes in the fence, fix them.
- Make sure you have no toxic plants in the garden.

The yard can be a dangerous place for your puppy. Chemical fertilizers and insecticides on your lawn are toxic.

Exercise

A Boxer does not need as much exercise as you may imagine. Of course, he loves to run, but he does not need to be in an area the size of a national park to keep trim and happy. Your first consideration must be his safety while he is loose. That is one reason why an enclosed backyard is such a great place—he can play safely there for hours.

A Boxer also does surprisingly well as an apartment dweller in the city—as long as he goes on two or three brisk walks a day and has a lot of human companionship so that he does not become utterly bored with his life.

You will find that puppies, like children, play hard and then sleep deeply. This is perfectly normal. Do not let the children constantly rouse the puppy from his naps. Naps are necessary for his well-being.

Good Routines = Good Habits

It is wise to accustom your puppy to a routine: meals at certain times of the day, walks immediately thereafter, and retiring for the night at a given hour. This schedule will foster good and lasting habits.

Everyone in the family should be committed to keeping to your puppy's schedule. The better everyone knows and encourages the routine, the sooner your puppy will be housetrained and the calmer he'll be because he'll know what to expect from you—and when. Plan a schedule that works for everyone in the family, but most importantly, for the puppy.

Whoever gets up first should let the puppy out to relieve himself. Soon thereafter, the puppy should get his morning meal; then it's right back outside to go to the bathroom again. (See chapter 10 for guidance on housetraining.)

Someone should play with the puppy for awhile and then put the pup in his crate for a nap. Later in the morning, puppy will need to go out again, eat, go out again, play, nap, go out again, perhaps nap, get his evening meal, go out again, and so on. You and your family can determine what times will be mealtimes and then schedule exercise, play, and naps around them.

Cropping and Docking

When you purchase your Boxer, his tail will undoubtedly have been docked. This operation is performed within a few days of birth. It is wise to be sure your puppy is docked, because the fast wagging long tail of the undocked Boxer can easily become bruised, cut, and infected.

Many owners prefer the alert look of the erect, cropped ear. Ear cropping is commonly done between 7 and 12 weeks of age. If you do plan to have the ears cropped, I recommend buying the puppy with this surgery already done. The

Puppies, like children, play hard and sleep deeply. Let sleeping dogs lie.

If you're going to crop your dog's ears, work with a knowledgeable breeder and an experienced veterinarian.

breeder is then responsible for making sure the ears heal properly, a process that takes about two weeks. After healing, the ears are then taped upright until they stand properly. This process can take many weeks—*sometimes more than a year.*

The breeder should help and instruct you in the proper methods of taping ears. It is *not,* unfortunately, a task that offers instant gratification. *Be patient;* the most common reason for ear failures is that the owners gave up too soon.

If the cropping is your responsibility, consult knowledgeable breeders so that you choose a veterinarian who is skilled in the procedure. Not only must they know how to do the surgery, but you must make certain that they use appropriate anesthesia for a young puppy.

Many owners choose not to crop their puppy's ears. It is a matter of personal preference. This is perfectly acceptable under the breed standard.

Chapter 6

Feeding Your Boxer

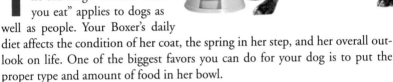

T he old adage "You are what you eat" applies to dogs as well as people. Your Boxer's daily diet affects the condition of her coat, the spring in her step, and her overall outlook on life. One of the biggest favors you can do for your dog is to put the proper type and amount of food in her bowl.

About Nutrition

There are six staples of nutrition that dogs need every day: protein, carbohydrates, fats, vitamins, minerals, and water. Following is a summary of what these provide your dog and why they're necessary. Remember, nutrition is a science, and this is the briefest of discussions. Commercial dog food manufacturers spend millions of dollars to make sure their products contain the proper amounts of each nutrient category (except water, which you must provide for your dog). There are many books that go into the subject in more detail.

Protein is used for bone growth, tissue repair, and the daily replacement of body tissues used by a normally active dog. Sources of protein include meat and eggs. Protein is not stored in your dog's body, so it must be replaced every day.

Carbohydrates provide energy, help assimilate fats, and aid digestion and elimination. Sources of carbohydrates include grains such as wheat, rice, soy, and corn. Carbohydrates break down into starches and sugars to provide the body with energy-efficient fuel. Excess carbohydrates are stored in the body for future use.

Water!

Supplying your puppy or adult dog with fresh water is one of the most important things you can do to ensure her long-term health. Our own and our canine's bodies are made up of more than 66 percent water. Therefore, we need to renew this simple compound continually.

While a human is supposedly intelligent enough to consume water in a variety of ways, your dog depends on her water bowl. It should be available to her almost twenty-four hours a day. Insufficient water intake leads to a variety of serious medical conditions. One of the most common is kidney failure in adult dogs. In very young puppies, dehydration is a more immediate danger. Regular access to fresh water in a clean dish cannot be overemphasized.

Fats are another necessary energy source. They also provide shine and suppleness to your dog's coat. But, as we all know too well, excess fat is not good for us or for our dogs. It leads to obesity and associated health problems. Getting too little fat is equally harmful, however, so maintaining a balance is important.

Vitamins contribute to numerous cellular and hormonal functions, including digestion, reproduction, and growth. Vitamins are necessary for releasing nutrients from food. They are not synthesized within the body, and must be acquired from foods or supplements. Let's look at some of the vitamins that are necessary for the health of your Boxer. (Please consult your veterinarian if you want to supplement your dog's food with any vitamins.)

Vitamin A is necessary for a healthy, shiny coat because it is used by your dog's body for fat absorption. It is also essential for normal growth rate, reproduction, and good eyesight.

The B vitamins protect the nervous system and are also important for healthy skin, appetite, eyes, and growth.

Vitamin C has been called a wonder vitamin for its immune-boosting and other healing properties. It is one of the primary antioxidants. Studies are constantly being conducted on the properties of vitamin C, and some dog owners add it to their dog's food for the same reasons they take it themselves. What the body cannot use is excreted in the urine.

Vitamin D, "the sunshine vitamin," is essential for healthy bones, teeth, and muscles, but must work in conjunction with the minerals calcium and phosphorus.

Vitamin E contributes to the proper functioning of the internal and reproductive organs, as well as the muscles.

Minerals are in the tissues of all living things, contributing to bones, muscles, cells, nerves, and blood. Like vitamins, minerals work together and individually. Essential minerals include calcium, phosphorus, cobalt, copper, chlorine, iodine, iron, magnesium, manganese, sodium, and zinc.

Water is perhaps the most important nutrient of all, for without it, cellular functions would cease and life would end.

3 to 6 Months Old

When you bring your new puppy home from her breeder's kennel, you will undoubtedly have been given a written summary of her diet to date. *Do not change* the puppy's diet regimen—at least not until she is well established in your household. Baby puppies have sensitive digestive tracts, and a sudden change in food may cause them either to stop eating or develop diarrhea—both unpleasant.

Don't change your baby puppy's food right away. Feed her what her breeder gave her, and, if you want to, very gradually change her diet.

Most veterinarian-approved books on puppy care will advise you to feed an 8-week-old pup up to four times a day. I find that three times daily at that age is sufficient, and by the time my puppies are 12 weeks old, I have them accustomed to a twice-daily schedule. They appear to thrive, and in fact they remain on this regimen for the rest of their lives.

Scheduling is very important. Your puppy should become accustomed to a routine that is comfortable for her household. If you constantly change the time and location of her feedings, you will encourage a fussy and frustrated eater. Your dog should have her own special place where she consumes every meal—usually in the kitchen. Many owners feed their dog inside the crate, especially if there are other dogs in the household who might just try to steal a few mouthfuls.

We do not feed the higher protein puppy foods beyond the age of about 4 months. At that time we switch permanently to a good-quality adult maintenance food. This adult dry food contains 23 percent protein and 14 percent fat; yours may be different. Remember that Boxers are sometimes susceptible to osteodystrophy, a bone disease of fast-growing dogs causing lameness and pain. While this can be bacterial in origin, evidence suggests that excessive protein levels in the food may contribute significantly to the development of this condition.

What to Feed Your Puppy

What should you feed your puppy? Although you should initially follow the breeder's advice, you will eventually settle on a diet of your own choosing. The availability of various brands may influence your choices. However, the best barometer of what to feed your growing dog is the animal herself. Is she robust and happy? Is her coat shiny? Is her overall health excellent? Are her stools firm? If so, you must be on the right track. Nonetheless, some recommendations based on long experience may prove helpful.

About Kibble

For most of us, the mainstay of a puppy's diet—and, indeed, of her adult diet—is the dry food or kibble you feed. There are as many brand names as there are dog breeds, and making a choice can be confusing.

One of the first things you should learn to do is to read a dog food label. Label ingredients are listed in descending order by weight. Therefore, the first item on the list makes up the heaviest volume. If you see chicken or lamb first on the list, however, remember that meat contains up to 75 percent moisture, so it may make up only a small fraction of the entire dry food. The label will go on to list every other component in the food, including minerals, vitamins, and preservatives.

Labels can be misleading, and no reference is made to the actual nutritional value of the ingredients. For example, there may be a considerable difference in quality of protein derived from chicken breasts and that derived from chicken feet.

TIP

Remember that the Boxer is not a naturally flatulent dog. Too much gas is a sign that the food is wanting.

Nonetheless, you will find that a study of labels can be enlightening. They vary considerably among manufacturers. In addition to the actual ingredients, the packaging will indicate percentages of protein, fat, fiber, and moisture as contained in the dry food overall.

You will find that most brands of good-quality kibble will meet or exceed the minimums set by the American Association of Feed Control Officials (AAFCO). In fact, my own chosen brand of puppy food is made up of 32 percent protein, 21 percent fat, 4 percent fiber, and 10 percent moisture. Yours may be different.

No Treats for Meals

When you have settled on a food that your puppy likes and that is optimally nutritious, do not allow yourself to be manipulated by your dog into substituting special treats for his regular meals. My husband grew up with a mixed breed dog who trained her family to feed her nothing but canned food and chicken gizzards—hardly an ideal diet!

Food should be left down for about thirty minutes and then removed until the next regular feeding. Don't worry—the chances of your finicky eater starving herself to death are minimal. Be strong!

How Much and How to Feed

In general, you will probably feed a growing Boxer puppy (between 8 and 16 weeks of age) between three and four cups of kibble daily. Of course, this amount will vary considerably with the individual puppy's metabolism, her rate of activity, and the amount of any additional foods you may include in her diet. Use your eyes and your common sense. Your puppy should not be fat; she should be lean and well-muscled. If you are looking at an animal in optimum condition, you are feeding appropriate foods.

We always feed our kibble soaked briefly in warm water. We begin this practice immediately upon weaning and maintain it throughout the puppy months and adult years. I have always believed that a soaked kibble promotes better digestibility, as it expands in the dish, not in the stomach. In

Reading Dog Food Labels

Dog food labels are not always easy to read, but if you know what to look for they can tell you a lot about what your dog is eating.

- The label should have a statement saying the dog food meets or exceeds the American Association of Feed Control Officials (AAFCO) nutritional guidelines. If the dog food doesn't meet AAFCO guidelines, it can't be considered complete and balanced, and can cause nutritional deficiencies.
- The guaranteed analysis lists the minimum percentages of crude protein and crude fat and the maximum percentages of crude fiber and water. AAFCO requires a minimum of 18 percent crude protein for adult dogs and 22 percent crude protein for puppies on a dry matter basis (that means with the water removed; canned foods will have less protein because they have more water). Dog food must also have a minimum of 5 percent crude fat for adults and 8 percent crude fat for puppies.
- The ingredients list the most common item in the food first, and so on until you get to the least common item, which is listed last.
- Look for a dog food that lists an animal protein source first, such as chicken or poultry meal, beef or beef byproducts, and that has other protein sources listed among the top five ingredients. That's because a food that lists chicken, wheat, wheat gluten, corn, and wheat fiber as the first five ingredients has more chicken than wheat, but may not have more chicken than all the grain products put together.
- Other ingredients may include a carbohydrate source, fat, vitamins and minerals, preservatives, fiber, and sometimes other additives purported to be healthy.
- Some grocery store brands may add artificial colors, sugar, and fillers—all of which should be avoided.

addition to water, I usually add a few tablespoons of canned dog food or raw hamburger to enhance palatability—but remember, the greatest nutritional value comes from the kibble, not the can. While you could feed your dog nothing but nutritionally complete canned food, most breeders prefer the dry foods. They are also (usually) more economical, and I find that they give a firmer stool—always a consideration when you are picking up after your dog!

6 to 12 Months of Age

During this transitional time, your puppy is growing taller and is beginning to fill out. When your Boxer is 10 to 12 months old, you will have some indication of what her adult body type will be. Some dogs mature early, others not until they are older—like people.

Feeding the rapidly growing and maturing puppy presents special challenges. You will be adjusting her food quantity to take into account her general condition and rate of growth.

Diet Do's and Don'ts

Sooner or later, someone is going to ask you what kind of vitamin-mineral supplement you are including in your puppy's diet. We do not supplement our growing puppies in pill, capsule, or powder form. Doing so is often very upsetting to the natural balance of the diet—sometimes to the considerable detriment of the pup.

Many years ago, I sold a young puppy to an intelligent and caring couple. Until I visited them in their home on the opposite coast, I did not realize that their pantry shelves were stocked with every mineral supplement known to humanity. Not only did they feed these supplements to themselves, they also fed them to their puppy, Chula—in great quantities. Not surprisingly, Chula developed a skeletal abnormality related to improper levels of calcium and phosphorous. None of her littermates were so afflicted, nor any of her relatives. Luckily, when we were able to re-home her, her developmental problems vanished. She grew up to be a sound adult and she lived well into her teens. I thought it a lesson well-learned, and I have discouraged all artificial supplementation in puppies from that day to this.

It is my belief that we can do much more harm than good by tampering with the carefully formulated ingredients in the food we have so conscientiously selected. We are certainly aware, however, that growing puppies need good-quality

It's hard to resist those little begging eyes, but it's better for your dog if she gets used to eating regular, nutritious meals from her own bowl.

Pet Food vs. People Food

Many of the foods we eat are excellent sources of nutrients—after all, we do just fine on them. But dogs, just like us, need the right combination of meat and other ingredients for a complete and balanced diet, and a bowl of meat doesn't provide that. In the wild, dogs eat the fur, skin, bones, and guts of their prey, and even the contents of the stomach.

This doesn't mean your dog can't eat what you eat. A little meat, dairy, bread, some fruits, or vegetables as a treat are great. Fresh foods have natural enzymes that processed foods don't have. Just remember, we're talking about the same food you eat, not the gristly, greasy leftovers you would normally toss in the trash. Stay away from sugar, too, and remember that chocolate is toxic to dogs.

If you want to share your food with your dog, be sure the total amount you give her each day doesn't make up more than 15 percent of her diet, and that the rest of what you feed her is a top-quality complete and balanced dog food. (More people food could upset the balance of nutrients in the commercial food.)

Can your dog eat an entirely homemade diet? Certainly, if you are willing to work at it. Any homemade diet will have to be carefully balanced, with all the right nutrients in just the right amounts. It requires a lot of research to make a proper homemade diet, but it can be done. It's best to work with a veterinary nutritionist.

calcium to promote proper skeletal development. Therefore, I often add foods that are *naturally* rich in calcium to the pup's routine feedings. These foods include cottage cheese and plain yogurt—easily digested and tasty besides. As long as the pup is an excellent eater, it is perfectly appropriate to offer other naturally good foods. For example, my pups and adults love bananas and cantaloupes!

Good Eating Habits

While you are developing your pup's good eating habits, there are a number of other things to consider. *Do not* feed the dog from your table unless you want a dog annoying you every time you sit down to a meal. What is appealing in a young puppy is decidedly aggravating in an adolescent or an adult who weighs fifty to seventy pounds and plops her paws on your lap while begging with her eyes.

And while we're mentioning table discipline, remember *never* to feed your dog chocolate in any form. A chemical in chocolate (theobromine), especially concentrated in dark chocolate, is poisonous to dogs and can cause death or serious illness.

Young Boxers are growing rapidly, but that doesn't mean they need endless amounts of vitamins and minerals.

Many dogs also do not do well with certain people foods, although they cannot be considered poisonous. For example, I find that my own dogs do not digest potatoes. Others have found spicy foods to disagree with their dogs. You'll know when your dog doesn't take to one of your favorites.

Feeding Raw Food

In recent years a growing number of people have decided to feed their dogs a diet made up almost entirely of raw or natural ingredients—either ordered from a commercial supply house specializing in this type of food (usually frozen in rolls) or by formulating their own diet for their individual dog. These diets might include raw chicken necks and backs, turkey, chopped vegetables, raw hamburger, raw eggs—there are countless formulations. Specific vitamins are also added.

Many Boxers thrive on raw food. The devotees of the raw diet believe it is healthier for the immune system and easier on the dog's digestive tract. One of the most popular of the raw diets is known as BARF (bones and raw food diet). For me, it makes sense to try to strike a balance between strictly raw and strictly processed foods. You can find information upon which to make your own assessments at www.barfworld.com.

Be Cautious

The pet food recalls of 2007 presented all of us with special challenges in feeding our dogs. Many of those widely advertised dog food companies that had been considered reliable were found to use imported grain ingredients from China that had clearly not been checked for toxicity—many animals died as a result.

To that end, I changed my own brand of dog food to be sure it was entirely American and/or Canadian made—that all the ingredients were grown *and* processed in these countries. Other consumers decided to feed entirely raw. We all made choices that we believed were the best for our Boxers. Future vigilance is clearly warranted.

The Adult and Aging Boxer

Feeding your adult dog is a matter of maintaining all the good nutritional practices you established when she was a puppy. You will adjust quantities depending on her mature physical size and the amount of food you need to maintain your Boxer's good health—and condition—the same way you fed her when she was a puppy. As time goes on, if you are faced with specific medical conditions, your vet may recommend special diets: foods formulated to aid failing kidneys, or volatile intestines, or the geriatric heart.

You will undoubtedly find that the aging dog will need less food than she did in the prime of her life. Her metabolism will slow down with the years. Likewise, if your Boxer suffers any tooth loss or gum deterioration as she grows older, you may increase the moisture content of her food so that she finds it easier to swallow. Remember that it is unhealthy for dogs as well as people to be overweight, and keeping your Boxer lean and trim as she ages is an important factor in promoting wellness.

The dog is an omnivore—that is, she eats and uses both animal and vegetable matter. Even the wolf and wild dogs of Africa demonstrate this biological fact by first consuming the stomachs and intestines of the grass-eating herbivores who make up the mainstay of their natural wild food. Balance between animal and

For optimum health, keep your dog trim as he ages. That may mean cutting back a bit on his portions.

vegetable matter in the domesticated dog's diet is the key to success in raising a happy and healthy canine, whether it be a Boxer or one of her predator wild cousins. If you maintain your Boxer on these scientifically formulated and balanced foods, supply her with fresh water for her entire life, encourage sensible exercise, and apply common sense liberally, you should find yourself with a healthy, gracefully aging dog who looks younger than her years.

Chapter 7

Grooming Your Boxer

Grooming your Boxer, as you might imagine, is not complicated. Affectionately known as "wash and wear" dogs, they require no involved grooming procedures. The requirements for keeping your Boxer clean and happy are simple.

You will find it helpful to train your Boxer from puppyhood to stand quietly while you are performing simple grooming tasks. If you are able to work in one particular area of your home, your Boxer will quickly become accustomed to his routine. While it's not necessary, buying a grooming table with a sturdy, non-skid surface on strong metal legs will be easiest on your own back and eyes, and will tell your Boxer wherever you go that it is time for his regular grooming sessions. These tables fold up and can be easily packed in the car when you are traveling with your dog. Some of them come with a metal arm and a nylon loop through which the dog's head is placed. Be sure never to leave him unattended even for a moment while he is restrained this way, in case he attempts to jump off the table.

Brushing

A Boxer's coat is short and sleek. It is the very devil to remove from clothing and upholstered surfaces, as the little hairs seem to have a willful desire to stick to the most unwelcome places. Your Boxer will shed these hairs with regularity, and if you live in an area with cold weather, he will shed almost his entire coat in what seems like a spring molt.

A curry comb (an oval brush made of hard rubber with rubber teeth) used in a circular motion will help you remove the dead hair before it ends up all over you and the upholstery. Be sure the curry is not too hard and that you apply it gently so as not to irritate sensitive skin. If your Boxer does not need to be curried, a soft brush is all that's necessary to keep him tidy. Brushing once a week is all that is needed to keep the Boxer's coat in optimum condition.

As you can see, grooming your Boxer is not complicated. These grooming sessions will be pleasurable for both you and your dog. It is also during these times that you

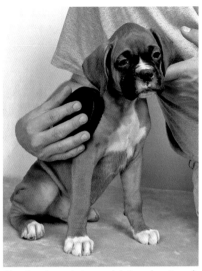

Your Boxer's coat is short and sleek, and won't need much care beyond weekly brushing.

may detect a small skin growth or a lump or bump that should not be there. Regular grooming is the first line of defense in detecting early cancers or benign skin conditions and treating them successfully. Likewise, if your dog develops hives as a result of allergies, or suffers from insect bites, you will be able to take appropriate measures. Careful attention to his appearance will help ensure his good health.

Bathing

Your Boxer will need very few baths each year. As we have mentioned earlier, he is a naturally clean animal, licking himself like a cat to keep himself spotless and polished. Excessive bathing will remove essential oils from your dog's coat and can result in skin irritation. Any minor surface dirt can be easily whisked away using a soft glove or a washcloth.

If circumstances demand a bath (for example, if your Boxer encountered a fully functioning skunk), you will want to make sure above all that your dog stays warm throughout the bathing process and does not become chilled. Choose a hot summer day to bathe him outdoors or use a heated bathroom for the procedure. Be sure to dry your dog thoroughly with clean towels or a hand-held human hair dryer set on warm, not hot. If warm weather cooperates, you can let the sun do its work as well.

Wet your dog thoroughly with *warm* water. Do not shock him with water that is too cold or too hot. Apply the shampoo conservatively and rub it gently into a lather. If you are using a shampoo that kills fleas or ticks, you will need to leave the lather in the coat for at least five minutes. Then rinse very thoroughly. Always follow label directions. If soap flakes dry on your dog's coat, they will look like unsightly dandruff. They can be rinsed away.

Always be careful to avoid getting soap in your dog's eyes. Likewise, try to keep water out of your Boxer's ears—remember, if he is cropped, he has no convenient ear flap to shed water. If you wish, you can gently swab the inside of the ears with cotton balls dampened with warm water or specially formulated ear cleaner. Do *not* go deep into the ear, as serious damage could be done to the delicate mechanisms within.

So Many Shampoos!

There seem to be as many shampoos on the market as there are breeds of dogs. The consumer is faced with an alluring array of choices: tea tree oil, oatmeal, high protein, whitening, baking soda, ginger, lanolin, apple, honeysuckle—you name it! Really, for your Boxer almost any one will do. Just be sure that the shampoo is specifically formulated for dogs and the special needs of their hair-coat—not for cats or gerbils or horses or people.

I prefer the simple cleansers that do one thing well—rid your pet of dirt. There are no magic formulas that do everything perfectly, but luckily, the Boxer does not require them. Unlike longhaired breeds that need conditioner for the coat to lie properly, the Boxer is happiest with any mild dog shampoo that does not to irritate his coat or his eyes.

If you are bathing the dog to kill fleas or ticks, be sure that your veterinarian approves of the insecticidal soap you use; some medicated shampoos are toxic not only to the parasites but to the dog as well! And always be especially vigilant when giving a puppy any medicated bath. At his young age, he may be especially sensitive to the chemicals contained in certain insecticidal shampoos.

Trimming Toenails

Regular monthly trimming of your dog's toenails is essential. Untrimmed nails lead to splayed feet and will cause your dog to slip on smooth surfaces. They also look terrible. If you begin gentle trimming when your puppy is young, you should have no trouble continuing to trim all through your Boxer's adult life.

Your puppy's breeder undoubtedly trimmed nails from the very earliest weeks in the whelping box, so your Boxer may already know the routine. Remember

New Products in the Fight Against Fleas

At one time, battling fleas meant exposing your dog and your-self to toxic dips, sprays, powders, and collars. But today there are flea preventives that work very well and are safe for your dog, you, and the environment. The two most common types are insect growth regulators (IGRs), which stop the immature flea from developing or maturing, and adult flea killers. To deal with an active infestation, experts usually recommend a prod-uct that has both.

These next-generation flea fighters generally come in one of two forms:

- **Topical treatments or spot-ons.** These products are applied to the skin, usually between the shoulder blades. The product is absorbed through the skin into the dog's system. Among the most widely available spot-ons are Advantage (kills adult fleas and larvae), Revolution (kills adult fleas), Frontline (kills adult fleas), Frontline Plus (kills adult fleas and larvae, plus an IGR), K-9 Advantix (kills adult fleas and larvae), and BioSpot (kills adult fleas and larvae, plus an IGR).
- **Systemic products.** This is a pill your dog swallows that transmits a chemical throughout the dog's bloodstream. When a flea bites the dog, it picks up this chemical, which then prevents the flea's eggs from developing. Among the most widely available systemic products are Program (kills larvae only, plus an IGR) and Capstar (kills adult fleas). I personally do not use such systemic preparations.

Make sure you read all the labels and apply the products exactly as recommended, and that you check to make sure they are safe for puppies. Consult your veterinarian for advice.

When the nail begins to look pink inside, stop cutting. (This is the guillotine type nail trimmer.)

too, if your Boxer has dewclaws on the insides of his front legs above the foot, these dewclaw nails also need regular trimming. Do not be confused if you cannot find them—they are most often removed on the same day as tail docking.

It will help to cut toenails outside on a sunny day. That way, you can hold the nail up to the light and see the quick—the small vein that runs about two-thirds the length of the nail. If you cannot see it, trim off just a bit of the nail tip at a time. When the nail begins to look pink inside, stop! Try to avoid cutting close to the quick, because the area is sensitive and your dog will tell you if you get too close. In addition to causing momentary discomfort to your dog, an overly aggressive approach will cause the nail to bleed. Do not despair; if you make this mistake, you must first apologize to your dog and then dip the nail in some commercially available variant of the familiar styptic powder used by most men who shave their whiskers every morning. In almost every instance, this powder will cause the bleeding to cease almost immediately. (If you don't have any handy, cornstarch will do.)

There are several nail-cutting tools available. One of these is the familiar guillotine type. Another looks like an ordinary scissors designed to fit easily around the nail. Professionals usually choose an electric nail grinder—an expensive but marvelous device. Whatever you choose should be comfortable for you and your Boxer. Be sure to keep blades sharp or replace them as necessary, depending on the tool you have chosen. If you use an electric grinder, be sure the speed is comfortable and that it does not build up too much heat around the nail.

This pup is getting his pedicure with an electric nail grinder.

If you're showing your dog, there are a few extra grooming steps—including trimming the whiskers.

Checking Teeth and Gums

Most Boxers do not require regular cleaning of the teeth until they reach middle to old age. However, it is prudent to check them periodically, just to be sure there are no injuries to the enamel or to the gums. If your dog's mouth is "smelly," he probably does need attention. It means retained and decaying food is stuck in his teeth and is causing the odor.

You can gently brush your Boxer's teeth with a soft toothbrush made for humans or a canine brush available at pet supply stores. You can use baking soda and water or one of the commercially available canine toothpastes especially for-mulated for dogs. Do not use human toothpastes, as they are unsuitable for the enamel of your Boxer's teeth. Do not be alarmed if you see an overgrowth of gum tissue in the older Boxer; this is most probably a benign condition called gingival hyperplasia that is rather common to the breed. (See chapter 8 for more information.)

If your Boxer has regular access to rubber, nylon, or rope chew toys, and if he gets occasional hard-baked food treats (biscuits), you will usually find that the simple stimulus of chewing keeps his mouth and teeth healthy and that tartar deposits will remain at a minimum.

Making Your Environment Flea Free

If there are fleas on your dog, there are fleas in your home, yard, and car, even if you can't see them. Take these steps to combat them.

In your home:

- Wash whatever is washable (the dog bed, sheets, blankets, pillow covers, slipcovers, curtains, etc.).
- Vacuum everything else in your home—furniture, floors, rugs, everything. Pay special attention to the folds and crevices in upholstery, cracks between floorboards, and the spaces between the floor and the baseboards. Flea larvae are sensitive to sunlight, so inside the house they prefer deep carpet, bedding, and cracks and crevices.
- When you're done, throw the vacuum cleaner bag away—in an outside garbage can.
- Use a nontoxic flea-killing powder, such as Flea Busters or Zodiac FleaTrol, to treat your carpets (but remember, it does not control fleas elsewhere in the house). The powder stays deep in the carpet and kills fleas (using a form of boric acid) for up to a year.
- If you have a particularly serious flea problem, consider using a fogger or long-lasting spray to kill any adult and larval fleas, or having a professional exterminator treat your home.

Grooming for the Show Ring

If you decide to exhibit your Boxer in conformation shows, grooming will take on another dimension. Although the procedure will still be relatively simple, a bath and a trim will be necessary before every show weekend. Extra steps include trimming the facial whiskers with a scissors or an electric trimmer, shaving the inside of the ears to present a sharper appearance, and shaving the underside of the tail and trimming the end to look neat.

Any stray hairs should also be trimmed from the end of the penile sheath in males, and, likewise, unwanted hairs on the belly of either sex should be gently shaved. Be careful with clippers: if you make a cosmetic mistake, it will be very visible on your shorthaired Boxer and will take some time to grow out.

In your car:

- Take out the floor mats and hose them down with a strong stream of water, then hang them up to dry in the sun.
- Wash any towels, blankets, or other bedding you regularly keep in the car.
- Thoroughly vacuum the entire interior of your car, paying special attention to the seams between the bottom and back of the seats.
- When you're done, throw the vacuum cleaner bag away—in an outside garbage can.

In your yard:

- Flea larvae prefer shaded areas that have plenty of organic material and moisture, so rake the yard thoroughly and bag all the debris in tightly sealed bags.
- Spray your yard with an insecticide that has residual activity for at least thirty days. Insecticides that use a form of boric acid are non-toxic. Some newer products contain an insect growth regulator (such as fenoxycarb) and need to be applied only once or twice a year.
- For an especially difficult flea problem, consider having an exterminator treat your yard.
- Keep your yard free of piles of leaves, weeds, and other organic debris. Be especially careful in shady, moist areas, such as under bushes.

External Parasites

External parasites live on the outside of your Boxer's body. They are called parasites because they need your dog for life—either for food or to continue their life cycle. Without your dog, these pests would die. Unfortunately, parasites can also cause your dog great discomfort, irritation, illness, and sometimes even death. It's very important that you examine your dog carefully for parasites whenever you groom him.

The Ubiquitous Flea

A flea is a bloodsucking insect. It carries disease and acts as an intermediate host to the tapeworm. It can jump great distances and readily attaches itself to a host

How to Get Rid of a Tick

Although the new generation of flea fighters are partially effective in killing ticks once they are on your dog, they are not 100 percent effective and will not keep ticks from biting your dog in the first place. During tick season (which, depending on where you live, can be spring, summer, and/or fall), examine your dog every day for ticks. Pay particular attention to your dog's neck, behind the ears, the armpits, and the groin.

When you find a tick, use a pair of tweezers to grasp the tick as close as possible to the dog's skin and pull it out using firm, steady pressure. Check to make sure you get the whole tick (mouth parts left in your dog's skin can cause an infection), then wash the wound and dab it with some antibiotic ointment. Watch for signs of inflammation.

Ticks carry very serious diseases that are transmittable to humans, so dispose of the tick safely. Never crush it between your fingers. Don't flush it down the toilet either, because the tick will survive the trip and infect another animal. Instead, use the tweezers to place the tick in a tight-sealing jar or plastic dish with a little alcohol, put on the lid, and dispose of the container in an outdoor garbage can. Wash the tweezers thoroughly with hot water and alcohol.

if one is available. Fleas need moisture and warmth to grow and multiply. Therefore, in seasonal climates they often do not pose a problem in the winter. In tropical climates or in heated interiors, they can be a problem *all year long*.

Flea bites cause local irritation. That's why your dog will scratch in an attempt to rid himself of these parasites. Some dogs are allergic to the saliva in flea bites and develop an acute hypersensitivity to fleas. They exhibit signs of intense itching and will constantly scratch and bite where fleas have bitten them. This self-mutilation can be a serious problem, and even a very few fleas can cause this severe flea allergy dermatitis.

Fleas are prodigious multipliers and may seem to be everywhere. Female fleas lay eggs that drop off and hatch into larvae resembling worms. These larvae become adult fleas. Unchecked, they may make your home unlivable, and will readily feed on you if you send your dog on a vacation.

Fleas are easy to see. They look like small, dark, moving specks. If the infestation is light, you may see only "flea dirt" on your Boxer's short coat. These tiny specks look like bits of dirt, but they're actually flea feces. If you moisten them, you will see the water become tinged red, because they contain blood. Common sites of infestation are at the scrotum and around and under the tail. In serious infestations, fleas may be found anywhere on the dog.

There are no easy solutions to controlling fleas. Not only the dog but also his environment must be treated. The box on pages 70–71 has some suggestions. Remember, however, that all flea-killing products contain toxic chemicals and must be used with caution. Always consult your veterinarian for professional advice. Pay particular attention to medications that affect young puppies. Personally, I do not use flea collars because there are many safer and more effective remedies. Diatomaceous earth, the fossilized remains of hard-shelled algae,

Fleas lurk everywhere outdoors and can be a serious problem. Protect your dog.

is nontoxic and useful for controlling fleas in your yard. When it is spread on the surface of the grass or dirt, the flea larvae are killed when their exoskeletons are punctured and the diatomaceous earth absorbs their body moisture, thereby dehydrating them. Diatomaceous earth is available in small or large quantities by the pound.

Ticks

Ticks are bloodsucking parasites. They are discouragingly hardy and are carriers for many diseases, including Rocky Mountain spotted fever, Lyme disease, ehrlichiosis, and encephalitis. They are found outdoors in high grass and wooded areas, and are adept at locating your dog. They can attach themselves anywhere, but have a preference for the insides of the ears. You may first notice them if your Boxer seems to be scratching at one particular spot. In addition, Boxers seem to have a specific skin sensitivity to certain tick bites. For example, ticks native to my New England area cause a raised welt around the bite, which is often my first warning of the tick embedded therein.

During the tick season, which can be any time the temperature is above freezing, you should examine your Boxer every day for ticks. Tick control products are available for the dog and the environment. As with those for fleas, consult your veterinarian and heed the potential toxicities of these chemicals.

Chapter 8

Keeping Your Boxer Healthy

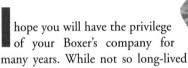

I hope you will have the privilege of your Boxer's company for many years. While not so long-lived as some breeds, Boxers, with good care, commonly live ten to twelve or more years. When health problems do arise, your dog's best line of defense is you—the loving, alert owner who will see to it that proper medical treatment is rendered early and effectively.

Choosing a Veterinarian

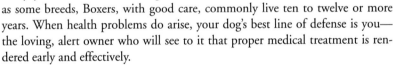

You will find that your choice of veterinarian is critical to your dog's good care. This practitioner must not only be skilled as a diagnostician and a surgeon, but must also be a good listener—to you, because you know your dog best. Beware the vet who never has time to talk to you or doesn't care what you have to say. Beware the vet who belittles your medical knowledge. The best medical professionals will be acutely interested in your observations and your insights.

To find a good veterinarian, seek recommendations from experienced breeders in your area. They will offer very definite opinions on whom you should trust in a time of crisis. They may know that a particular vet has a particular knowledge of or love for the Boxer breed. All this advice is helpful, but the final choice is yours. Be sure you have confidence in your vet, that he or she is medically skilled and is someone to whom you can relate.

Vaccines

What vaccines dogs need and how often they need them has been a subject of controversy for several years. Researchers, health care professionals, vaccine manufacturers, and dog owners do not always agree on which vaccines each dog needs or how often booster shots must be given.

In 2006, the American Animal Hospital Association issued a set of vaccination guidelines and recommendations intended to help dog owners and veterinarians sort through much of the controversy and conflicting information. The guidelines designate four vaccines as core, or essential for every dog, because of the serious nature of the diseases and their widespread distribution. These are canine distemper virus (using a modified live virus or recombinant modified live virus vaccine), canine parvovirus (using a modified live virus vaccine), canine adenovirus-2 (using a modified live virus vaccine), and rabies (using a killed virus). The general recommendations for their administration (except rabies, for which you must follow local laws) are:

- Vaccinate puppies at 6–8 weeks, 9–11 weeks, and 12–14 weeks.
- Give an initial "adult" vaccination when the dog is older than 16 weeks; two doses, three to four weeks apart, are

Preventive Health Care

Your Boxer's first line of defense against illness is you, the caregiver who sees her daily. You must be alert to any signs that might indicate a deviation from the usual state of health. Often, before your veterinarian can make a definitive diagnosis of trouble, you may notice subtle changes that might escape the notice of anyone who does not live with your dog. Perhaps your Boxer seems slightly less enthusiastic about her food, seems to be drinking more water than usual, or just doesn't want to engage in her usual play activities. Trust your instincts; follow up advised, but one dose is considered protective and acceptable.

- Give a booster shot when the dog is 1 year old.
- Give a subsequent booster shot every three years, unless there are risk factors that make it necessary to vaccinate more or less often.

Noncore vaccines should only be considered for those dogs who risk exposure to a particular disease because of geographic area, lifestyle, frequency of travel, or other issues. They include vaccines against distemper-measles virus, canine parainfluenza virus, leptospirosis, Bordetella bronchiseptica, and Borrelia burgdorferi (Lyme disease).

Vaccines that are not generally recommended because the disease poses little risk to dogs or is easily treatable, or the vaccine has not been proven to be effective, are those against giardia, canine coronavirus, and canine adenovirus-1.

Often, combination injections are given to puppies, with one shot containing several core and noncore vaccines. Your veterinarian may be reluctant to use separate shots that do not include the noncore vaccines, because they must be specially ordered. If you are concerned about these noncore vaccines, talk to your vet.

on your suspicions with a closer look, and if your dog does not quickly resume her normal behavior patterns, seek professional help.

Routine Checkups

It is sound medical advice to take your Boxer to the veterinarian for routine examinations—every six months for a younger dog, and at least once a year for a normal adult. The veterinarian will listen to your dog's heart for any irregularities and will check her thoroughly. He may pick up an abnormality apparent to only his professional eyes and ears. Fecal checks for internal parasites can also be done at this time.

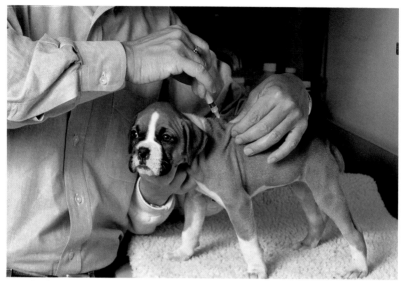

Your dog's breeder should tell you what shots she has already had.

Internal Parasites

A variety of internal parasites can infect your Boxer, both as a puppy and as an adult. Fortunately, many can be prevented by scrupulous attention to hygiene. If your dog does become afflicted, there are effective, safe medications to eliminate the parasite from your pet. Remember, most of these medications are *potentially toxic*; they must be dosed with care. This warning includes the so-called "all natural" products.

Always consult your veterinarian for the proper drugs and *do not* casually administer over-the-counter remedies, which may not work for the problem your dog has. Fecal examinations are used to identify any specific parasite; therefore, routine checks are advisable.

Roundworms (Ascarids)

Roundworms are a common parasite, especially in puppies. Signs of infection include a failure to thrive, dull coat, and a pot belly. Your dog may have mucus-like diarrhea and pneumonia (due to migrating larvae in the lungs). Roundworm eggs are ingested by eating infected soil and feces, and can be transmitted to people. Despite all a breeder's best efforts, many pups are born with a roundworm infection acquired from the mother before the pup is born.

Why Spay and Neuter?

Breeding dogs is a serious undertaking that should only be part of a well-planned breeding program. Why? Because dogs pass on their physical and behavioral problems to their offspring. Even healthy, well-behaved dogs can pass on problems in their genes.

Is your dog so sweet that you'd like to have a litter of puppies just like her? If you breed her to another dog, the pups will not have the same genetic heritage she has. Breeding her *parents* again will increase the odds of a similar pup, but even then, the puppies in the second litter could inherit different genes. In fact, *there is no way to breed a dog to be just like another dog*.

Meanwhile, thousands and thousands of dogs are killed in animal shelters every year simply because they have no homes. Casual breeding is a big contributor to this problem.

If you don't plan to breed your dog, is it still a good idea to spay her or neuter him? Yes!

When you spay your female:

- You avoid her heat cycles, during which she discharges blood and scent.
- It greatly reduces the risk of mammary cancer and eliminates the risk of pyometra (an often fatal infection of the uterus) and uterine cancer.
- It prevents unwanted pregnancies.
- It reduces dominance behaviors and aggression.

When you neuter your male:
- It curbs the desire to roam and to fight with other males.
- It greatly reduces the risk of prostate cancer and eliminates the risk of testicular cancer.
- It helps reduce leg lifting and mounting behavior.
- It reduces dominance behaviors and aggression.

It is not uncommon to see roundworms in your dog's stool. They are stringy and white, and may be elongated or coiled. In severe infestations, a puppy may vomit the worms. Since an adult female roundworm may lay 200,000 eggs daily, early detection and elimination are essential.

Hookworms

Hookworms live in the small intestine and exert their influence on the host by attaching to the intestinal wall and sucking blood. As they move to new feeding sites, the old wounds they have caused ulcerate and continue to bleed. Thus, a puppy heavily infected with hookworms may develop severe anemia. Pale gums, dark and tarry diarrhea, weakness, and emaciation are all clinical signs. Transfusions may be necessary in severe infestations. Adult dogs may harbor a chronic infection with less dramatic symptoms. Recovery is rapid after appropriate treatment.

Tapeworms

These parasites are transmitted to the dog by the intermediate host, the flea. They can be up to seventy centimeters long, and segments resembling grains of rice may be passed in the feces. Tapeworms cause general failure to thrive, colic, mild diarrhea, and occasional loss of appetite. Flea control (see chapter 7) is important to interrupt the life cycle of the worm.

There's no way to breed a dog who is exactly like another dog.

Whipworms

Whipworms are sometimes difficult to detect in fecal exams because they shed their eggs only intermittently. Repeated testing may be necessary. Adult whipworms live in the cecum, a pouch in the large intestine. Signs in a light infestation are minimal, but severe infections produce weight loss, a poor coat, and diarrhea that is often streaked with fresh blood. Whipworm eggs will not survive in dry areas, and regular cleaning of any moist spots in the yard or kennel run will help control infestations.

Heartworms

Heartworm disease is a serious con-dition that is often fatal without treatment. The worm itself is trans-mitted in larval form by the bite of infected mosquitoes. Adult worms live in the heart muscle and cause symptoms related to circulatory dis-turbances, including weakness, coughing, intolerance to exercise, respiratory distress, weight loss, and sudden death.

Heartworm disease can be pre-vented by daily or monthly doses of appropriate medication throughout the mosquito season and for two months thereafter. In some parts of the country, veterinarians advise that dogs be kept on heartworm pre-ventive year-round. Before begin-

Worms are very common in puppies, even when they are well taken care of. Make sure your veteri-narian checks your pup for worms.

ning any heartworm medication, your dog should get a blood test to check that there are no worms already in her body. All these preparations can be toxic, and seizures resulting from the monthly meds are, unfortunately, not unknown, although they are not common.

Coccidia

Coccidia are protozoan parasites that live in the intestines. They most com-monly affect puppies. Symptoms include bloody diarrhea, emaciation, and dehydration. Proper sanitation is critical. The infection clears up easily with medication.

Giardia

This protozoal disease infects mammals and birds. The parasites live in the small intestines and are acquired when cysts are ingested from contaminated water. Symptoms include chronic diarrhea, which may be intermittent, as well as weight loss. The feces are sometimes greasy and soft. Prompt diagnosis and treatment is curative.

Lyme disease can be lurking in your own backyard. Check your dog regularly for ticks.

Lyme Disease

This tick-borne disease is widespread throughout North America. It is caused by a spirochete, *Borrelia burgdorferi,* and is transmitted primarily by the deer tick, although it's suspected that other ticks may carry the spirochete as well. Intermediate hosts include deer, mice, and other rodents.

Symptoms usually come on rapidly. They include depression, fever in the range of 103 to 105 degrees Fahrenheit, loss of appetite, joint swelling, and often severe pain in the limbs and/or back. This pain may migrate from one site to another. Migrating leg lameness makes most veterinarians suspect Lyme disease.

Not all symptoms will appear in every case, and thus Lyme disease is difficult to diagnose and is often mistaken for other problems. Your veterinarian must be alert to the possibility of Lyme in your area and take appropriate measures. These include blood testing for the disease. However, a negative test does not necessarily mean Lyme can be ruled out, because early infections do not always cause a positive titer result.

Specific antibiotic therapy early in the course of infection will cure most cases of Lyme disease, but misdiagnosis and lack of appropriate treatment can eventually lead to fatal complications. Unfortunately, successful treatment does not bring immunity, and your Boxer will be susceptible again if she is bitten by another infected tick.

Home Health Care

Your canine medicine cabinet should contain gauze pads and cloth bandages—all to be used in either routine or emergency situations. Be sure you know where these items are so that you can get them quickly if the situation warrants. Make sure one of the bandage strips can serve as a muzzle if you need it. See the box on page 85 for other items you should have on hand. Ask your veterinarian for specific recommendations if you have questions.

Do not buy over-the-counter preparations without checking with your vet first. Some may be dangerous to your Boxer. They include, but are not limited to, aspirin and other analgesics, "worm" medicines, and flea and tick products.

Giving Your Dog Medication

You can hide pills in hamburger or another tasty treat and easily feed them to most Boxers. Failing that, you can open the dog's jaws with one hand while pushing the pill gently down the gullet with the other. Massage the throat to encourage swallowing, and make sure the dog does not spit out the medicine. Quickly following up with a tasty treat is helpful.

Liquid medications can be squirted carefully and slowly into the rear side pocket formed by the Boxer's pendulous lips. Open the jaws with one hand, raise the head slightly, and administer the liquid, giving the dog time to swallow.

To apply eye ointment or drops, face your dog and carefully pull down the lower eyelid. This action will cause a pocket to form between the lid and the eyeball. Squeeze or drip the appropriate medication into this pocket, and release the lower lid. The medication will be dispersed over the surface of the eye.

Your dog relies on you to make sure she gets the care she needs.

Taking Your Dog's Temperature

One of the most important items you should own is a simple rectal thermometer that is just for your dog. It can be digital or the old-fashioned mercury thermometer if you have one. While a normal temperature is not necessarily an indicator of good health, an elevated or subnormal temperature may indicate certain problems. Your Boxer's normal temperature will be in the range of 100.5 to 102.5 degrees Fahrenheit. Any routine call to your vet for help should include a fresh reading of your dog's temperature.

Taking this reading is quite simple. Lubricate the end of the thermometer with some petroleum jelly so that it can be inserted gently into the rectum. Leave it in place for a minute or two. Put your hand under your dog's tummy to

> **TIP**
>
> Your dog's normal heart rate, depending on her recent activity, should be 70 to 160 beats per minute. Her respiratory rate should be 10 to 30 breaths per minute at rest.

encourage her to stand. Keep a string attached to it or hold onto it while it's inside your dog so that it is not drawn into the rectum. After two minutes, withdraw it, wipe it off, and read it. Your Boxer may find the process slightly uncomfortable, but most dogs will allow you to perform your task without serious protest.

Emergencies

If your dog has been in a serious accident or encountered a serious trauma, you must first analyze the situation. Ask yourself these questions:

- Is your Boxer bleeding profusely?
- Are her gums pale and white, indicating shock or internal bleeding?
- Is there any obvious abnormality, such as a broken limb, severe contusions, or an obstructed airway?

The ability to assess these conditions quickly will enable you to perform what could be lifesaving emergency care.

Handling an Injured Dog

If your Boxer is in pain, no matter how much she loves you, she may bite if you try to handle her. Therefore, wind a strip of cloth (a stocking will do) around her muzzle, in back of the nose, and tie it in a half-knot. If you have

How to Make a Canine First-Aid Kit

If your dog hurts herself, even a minor cut, it can be very upsetting for both of you. Having a first-aid kit handy will help you to help her, calmly and efficiently. What should be in your canine first-aid kit?

- Antibiotic ointment
- Antiseptic and antibacterial cleansing wipes
- Benadryl
- Cotton-tipped applicators
- Disposable razor
- Elastic wrap bandages
- Extra leash and collar
- First-aid tape of various widths
- Gauze bandage roll
- Gauze pads of different sizes, including eye pads
- Hydrogen peroxide
- Instant cold compress
- Kaopectate tablets or liquid
- Latex gloves
- Lubricating jelly
- Muzzle
- Nail clippers
- Pen, pencil, and paper for notes and directions
- Pepto-Bismol
- Round-ended scissors and pointy scissors
- Safety pins
- Sterile saline eyewash
- Thermometer (rectal)
- Tweezers

time, make a second closed loop and pull so that it is under the jaw. Complete the procedure by tying a bow behind the ears. A muzzle will prevent the real potential of injury to you. Be sure it does not impede your dog's breathing.

If a blanket is available, try to slide it under your dog and carry her to safety or into your car for a trip to the vet. Your coat or a sweater may take the place of a blanket in an emergency. Try not to jostle the dog.

When to Call the Veterinarian

Go to the vet right away or take your dog to an emergency veterinary clinic if:

- Your dog is choking
- Your dog is having trouble breathing
- Your dog has been injured and you cannot stop the bleeding within a few minutes
- Your dog has been stung or bitten by an insect and the site is swelling
- Your dog has been bitten by a snake
- Your dog has been bitten by another animal (including a dog) and shows any swelling or bleeding
- Your dog has touched, licked, or in any way been exposed to a poison
- Your dog has been burned by either heat or caustic chemicals
- Your dog has been hit by a car
- Your dog has any obvious broken bones or cannot put any weight on one of her limbs
- Your dog has a seizure

Make an appointment to see the vet as soon as possible if:

- Your dog has been bitten by a cat, another dog, or a wild animal
- Your dog has been injured and is still limping an hour later

Emergency Resuscitation

The easiest way to check to see whether the heart is beating is by feeling for the femoral arterial pulse on the inside of your Boxer's upper rear legs. If you move your index finger down the femur (upper bone) and apply slight pressure, you should easily be able to feel the pulse. If the dog is not breathing but has a pulse, begin artificial respiration. If there is no pulse, begin cardiopulmonary resuscitation (CPR).

Artificial Respiration

If a dog is in danger of death from suffocation, you must immediately restore her airway if it is blocked. If she has been underwater and has stopped breathing, lift her by her hindquarters so that her head and neck hang vertical—you

- Your dog has unexplained swelling or redness
- Your dog's appetite changes
- Your dog vomits repeatedly and can't seem to keep food down, or drools excessively while eating
- You see any changes in your dog's urination or defecation (pain during elimination, change in regular habits, blood in urine or stool, diarrhea, foul-smelling stool)
- Your dog scoots her rear end on the floor
- Your dog's energy level, attitude, or behavior changes for no apparent reason
- Your dog has crusty or cloudy eyes, or excessive tearing or discharge
- Your dog's nose is dry or chapped, hot, crusty, or runny
- Your dog's ears smell foul, have a dark discharge, or seem excessively waxy
- Your dog's gums are inflamed or bleeding, her teeth look brown, or her breath is foul
- Your dog's skin is red, flaky, itchy, or inflamed, or she keeps chewing at certain spots
- Your dog's coat is dull, dry, brittle, or bare in spots
- Your dog's paws are red, swollen, tender, cracked, or the nails are split or too long
- Your dog is panting excessively, wheezing, unable to catch her breath, breathing heavily, or sounds strange when she breathes

are trying to drain fluids from her lungs. If you cannot lift her, lie her on her side so that her head is lower than her body and fluids can drain out. Now begin artificial respiration.

Exhaled air contains about 16 percent oxygen. This small amount is enough to sustain life in both people and dogs. Although the Boxer's short muzzle and nasal passages present special difficulties, mouth-to-muzzle breathing is possible. Clear the mouth of mucus and draw the tongue forward. Then close the muzzle with one hand, place your mouth over your dog's nostrils, and exhale. Remember to keep the dog's head extended. Watch your dog's chest: If she is getting air into her lungs, you will see a slight rise as you breathe the air into her. If the chest does not rise and fall and you think the nasal passages are blocked, try sealing the nose and breathing directly into the mouth.

CPR

CPR is a combination of heart massage and artificial respiration. For heart massage, place both hands, one on top of the other, over the region of the heart—where the elbow meets the ribs. Compress the chest using vigorous downward thrusts, about 100 compressions per minute. Check for a heartbeat about every thirty seconds.

Administering ten to fifteen rapid thrusts and one deep breath—repeated until help can arrive or you can get to a vet—will give your dog a chance. Your task will be much easier if two people are available—one to perform CPR and one to do artificial respiration. A ratio of one breath to four chest compressions is ideal.

These tasks are physically demanding—it is genuinely hard labor—but do not despair and do not give up until ten to fifteen minutes have passed with no response from your dog.

Bleeding

If blood is spurting from the dog in rhythmic bursts, an artery has undoubtedly been cut. If the wound involves an artery or a major vein, you must act quickly. Start by putting direct pressure on the wound. You can use a bandage, or your hand, or whatever works with what you have available. Keep pressure on the wound until the bleeding is under control, or until you can get your dog to the veterinarian.

Even the sweetest and gentlest dog can become dangerous when she is hurt and in pain. Handle your injured dog carefully.

If you absolutely cannot stop the bleeding, consider applying a tourniquet. You can make one using the dog's leash, your belt, or even by tearing off a strip of your clothing if nothing else is available. Place it above the wound, wrap it and pull it tight until the bleeding stops or lessens dramatically. You must be very careful with tourniquets: While they may save your dog's life, they also cut off circulation to the affected area and should be used with caution. Be sure to loosen the tourniquet briefly every few minutes.

Bloat

Bloat, the acute dilation of the stomach, occurs when the stomach fills with gas and air. This condition can be a life-threatening emergency. This swelling prevents the dog from vomiting or passing gas. Consequently, the pressure builds, cutting off blood from the heart and to other parts of the body. This causes shock or heart failure, either of which can cause death.

You may observe that suddenly your Boxer's abdomen looks very full and abnormally large. The dog may whine, salivate, and make unsuccessful attempts to vomit. Unfortunately, this distension often

Big dogs with wide chests are subject to bloat.

causes the stomach to twist on its long axis (a condition called gastric torsion), cutting off its circulation. Shock and death follow without surgical intervention.

If you suspect bloat and/or torsion, *do not waste time* getting your Boxer to your vet. This is a genuine emergency. To be successful, treatment should begin at once. In a simple case of bloat without torsion, the condition may be relieved by passing a stomach tube to release the gaseous pressure. Gastric torsion requires surgery to return the stomach to its proper position.

Bloat and torsion are often associated with the rapid ingestion of a large meal or too much water, and vigorous exercise before or after eating or drinking. However, some dogs bloat for unknown reasons. It is prudent to feed your Boxer two meals a day so that she does not eat a huge quantity at any one time. We usually restrict exercise for at least one hour after a meal. Frantic gulping of food, which causes the dog to swallow a lot of air, should be discouraged.

Choking

If your dog is choking or unconscious after unsuccessful efforts to cough up a foreign object, you must attempt the canine equivalent of the Heimlich maneuver. First, if you are able, reach deep into her throat to try to pull the object out. If you succeed and the dog is not breathing, proceed with artificial respiration and CPR. If you do not succeed in removing the object, lay the dog on her side and place your palms, one on top of the other, on the abdomen right below the rib cage. Administer a sharp, upward thrust to this area and repeat until the object is expelled. If these efforts fail, proceed with CPR.

Heatstroke

The short muzzle of the Boxer renders her particularly susceptible to heatstroke. She must never be left in a closed car in hot weather—even briefly. The interior of an unventilated automobile can become a death trap in just a few minutes. Even with the windows open, a Boxer is at risk. Likewise, she must not be left outside in the sun without shelter, nor permitted too much strenuous physical activity on hot days. Use your common sense.

Signs of heatstroke are related to very high internal temperature—up to 109 degrees Fahrenheit—a temperature that will result in rapid death if the condition is not treated immediately. A dog with heatstroke will have a weak and rapid pulse, pale and often grayish gums, and warm, dry skin. Some dogs vomit and have diarrhea.

If your dog is experiencing heatstroke, rapid cooling is in order. Do this with a cold water bath or by hosing her down. If she does not improve in a few minutes (ideally, check the rectal temperature every five minutes), you may give her a cold water enema, but rectal temperature readings will not be accurate if you do.

Be sensible about the weather. When it's hot out, keep your dog inside where it's cool. You can take her out at dawn and dusk.

ASPCA Animal Poison Control Center

The ASPCA Animal Poison Control Center has a staff of licensed veterinarians and board-certified toxicologists available 24 hours a day, 365 days a year. The number to call is (888) 426-4435. You will be charged a consultation fee of $60 per case, charged to most major credit cards. There is no charge for follow-up calls in critical cases. At your request, they will also contact your veterinarian. Specific treatment and information can be provided via fax. Put the number in large, legible print with your other emergency telephone numbers. Be prepared to give your name, address, and phone number; what your dog has gotten into (the amount and how long ago); your dog's breed, age, sex, and weight; and what signs and symptoms the dog is showing. You can log onto www.aspca.org and click on "Animal Poison Control Center" for more information, including a list of toxic and nontoxic plants.

Get your dog to a veterinarian immediately so she can receive additional treatment. But remember—get your Boxer's temperature down without delay. Speed is critical.

Poisoning

Your dog may be poisoned by a variety of substances, some obvious and some quite unexpected. The symptoms of poisoning are as varied as the toxic agents dogs sometimes ingest. They may include nausea, vomiting, bleeding from bodily orifices, seizures, convulsions, salivation, labored breathing, and collapse. No matter what time of day or night the poisoning occurs, call your veterinarian immediately.

The vet may tell you to induce vomiting. One teaspoon of hydrogen peroxide (3 percent strength or less) per ten pounds of body weight, or one tablespoon per thirty pounds, should be effective. The quickest way to get it into your dog is with a baster or a plastic syringe without the needle. If the dog has ingested certain poisons, such as caustic lye, acids, and petroleum products, vomiting should not be induced. That is why you should always consult your veterinarian.

Accidents can happen any time. Make sure you know what to do in an emergency.

Remember that many plants are poisonous to your dog. These include yew, amaryllis, nightshade, monkshood, daffodil bulbs, and a host of others. Household products such as shoe polish, mothballs, paint, dye, turpentine, antifreeze, and suntan lotion are toxic. Unfortunately, antifreeze is especially appealing to dogs. Many lawn fertilizers and weed killers are poisonous and can be ingested when the dog licks her paws. Years ago a friend sold a healthy puppy who was dead in a few days because the lawn had been treated with chlordane. Chocolate is poisonous to dogs and even in small amounts can prove fatal. If in doubt, call your vet and/or the poison control hotline (see the box on page 91). *Time is of the essence, so do not wait*—no matter what the hour of day or night.

Shock

Shock is a generalized, progressive failure of the circulatory system, usually due to trauma or overwhelming infection. Common signs of shock include labored breathing, a weak and rapid pulse, pale gums, cold extremities, and eventually, coma. Any time your Boxer has suffered severe trauma, she is in danger from shock and must be seen by a veterinarian immediately. Sometimes the shock syndrome can prove fatal even if the initial trauma is not.

Treatment involves intravenous fluids and other appropriate professional therapy. Be sure to keep your dog warm until medical help is available. Unless absolutely necessary, do not muzzle a dog in shock; her breathing may be too restricted.

Problems Affecting Boxers

Despite all our care and attention, our Boxers do occasionally suffer from conditions to which the breed seems to be predisposed. Of course, not all Boxers have these problems. But some do. Whether these illnesses are genetic in origin or occasioned by environmental factors, they need to be addressed.

Aortic Stenosis

Aortic stenosis is a congenital, genetic heart defect in which the dog has a narrowing or constriction of the outflow from the left ventricle to the aorta. Usually, this defect occurs below the aortic valve and thus is called subaortic stenosis (SAS). It can be detected as a systolic murmur by your veterinarian—often in a young puppy if the narrowing is severe, or in an older dog if the constriction is less acute. This murmur must be distinguished from other types of murmurs—often so-called innocent "flow" murmurs that disappear as a puppy grows.

> **CAUTION**
>
> **No Acepromazine!**
>
> Studies have shown that Boxers do *not* tolerate the most common tranquilizer/pre-anesthetic in veterinary medicine—acepromazine, aka "ace" (the brand name is Promace). It can cause dangerously low blood pressure, slow heartbeat, heart arrhythmias, respiratory problems, and collapse. *Tell your veterinarian!*

SAS can cause heart failure and/or sudden death, but mild forms may go undetected and are not incompatible with a normal life span. SAS can be diagnosed using an echocardiogram in the office of a good canine cardiologist. The doctor can actually see the function of the heart muscle on a monitor and calibrate the flow rate (the force with which blood enters the aorta).

There is no practical surgical treatment. If the condition results in ventricular arrhythmias (irregular heartbeats), medication is available to help control the arrhythmia.

Boxer Cardiomyopathy

Boxer cardiomyopathy (sometimes known as arrythmogenic right ventricular cardiomyopathy, or ARVC) is an electrical disturbance within the heart. It can

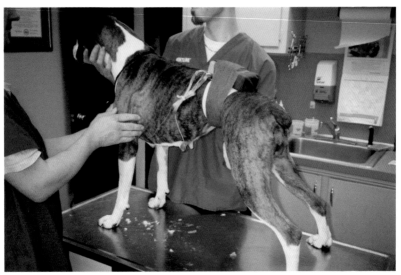

This Boxer is wearing a Holter monitor, used to test for Boxer cardiomyopathy.

precipitate life-threatening arrhythmias and often leads to sudden death or heart failure. It can be caused by certain poisons; bacterial, parasitic, and viral infections (notably parvovirus); severe uremia; diabetes; and heatstroke. In Boxers, however, it most often occurs in middle age and cannot be attributed to any known disease. Hereditary factors undoubtedly play a key role.

Boxer cardiomyopathy is widespread throughout the breed in North America, and there are no easy ways to avoid it. The good news is that there is a good chance your Boxer will never develop this condition. Nonetheless, you must be aware of its symptoms. If your Boxer ever displays a sudden weakness or faints, you must investigate the cause. If you are able, check for pale gums at the time of the incident. These are all classic Boxer cardiomyopathy signs in the breed, and they must not be ignored.

Often, if you take your dog to the vet after such an episode, her heart rhythm may be normal. Unfortunately, this is no guarantee of a healthy heart, because arrhythmias may only be detected upon stress in early stages of the disease. More sophisticated testing is required. A twenty-four-hour Holter monitor, recording each heartbeat during this period, is the best test we have at this time to diagnose the condition. Your veterinarian can refer you to a canine cardiologist to arrange for this monitor system—a simple small device strapped to your Boxer's midsection for the twenty-four hours.

Boxer cardiomyopathy can be treated with antiarrhythmic drugs, and once a dog's heart is properly regulated, she may live for years with no further symptoms. Conscientious Boxer breeders are funding research into this problem and hope one day to identify genetic markers so that Boxer cardiomyopathy can eventually be eliminated or greatly reduced in the breeding population.

ARVC is a unique form of the disease that is much more common in Boxers than other breeds for which cardiomyopathy is also a serious issue—such as the Doberman Pinscher.

Cancer

Boxers have been found to be at high risk for a large variety of tumors. These include both benign skin tumors (lipomas and histiocytomas) as well as cancers affecting the brain, skin, thyroid, mammary glands, testes, and internal organs such as the spleen and pancreas. Lymphoma (cancer of the lymph tissue) is not uncommon in the breed.

Benign skin tumors usually need either no treatment or simple surgical removal under local anesthesia. Malignancies require treatment specific to the

Sometimes the only sign of cancer will be a subtle change in your dog's behavior.

The American Boxer Charitable Foundation

The American Boxer Charitable Foundation (ABCF) was founded in 1995 to support research into medical conditions that specifically affect the Boxer. Working closely with the AKC Canine Health Foundation, which matches funds raised by the Boxer community for approved projects, the ABCF has to date raised more than $500,000 worldwide for our beloved Boxers—more than any other breed. The ABCF remains the largest single breed contributor to the Canine Health Foundation. For more information, or to donate, please go to www.abcfoundation.org.

cancer itself and vary widely. As in human cancers, dogs are treated with surgery, chemotherapy, and sometimes radiation. There have been tremendous advances made in canine treatment and survival times.

There is no way to predict whether your Boxer will develop any cancer as she ages. However, it is prudent to be alert to any unusual lumps, bumps, growths, or changes in her behavior. Consult your veterinarian if you observe anything suspicious.

Degenerative Myelopathy

This is a degenerative neurological disease affecting the spinal cord, and is most often seen in older Boxers. Typically, over a period of months, they lose control of their hindquarters. Eventually, they become incontinent. Most owners choose to euthanize the dog at this point, although there is no pain and the dogs can live long past the point where she can no longer walk.

Degenerative myelopathy has been known for decades, but only in the last ten to fifteen years has it become a notable problem in the breed. We shared our lives with a very beloved Boxer whom we kept with us for about a year after he could no longer support his weight in the rear. We "walked" him outside like a wheelbarrow and he adjusted very well, playing with his toys with his front feet and never missing a meal.

Unfortunately, then as now, there is no way known to medicine to halt the progress of this disease. The neurological deficit eventually affects the front legs and the strength of the neck. High doses of vitamin C and various natural supplements do not seem to help the Boxer as much as they do some other breeds that have this condition, notably the German Shepherd Dog. Some dogs adapt well to custom-made carts and learn to "walk" and trot again with such a device. We hope ongoing research will bring dogs and owners some much-needed optimism for the future.

Gingival Hyperplasia

These are benign tumors of the mouth, mainly overgrowth of gum tissue, and are commonly seen in middle-aged and older Boxers. These tumors may be numerous; however, they usually cause no significant harm. Occasionally, they distort the placement of the lips and are cosmetically unattractive. Since they may catch and hold food particles, you must pay special attention to oral hygiene. Always consult your veterinarian to rule out any potential malignancy.

Hip Dysplasia

Hip dysplasia is a failure of the head of the femur (thighbone) to properly fit into the acetabulum (hip socket). This is a developmental disease of the hip joint affecting many breeds, including Boxers. The joint weakens and loses proper function. Reluctance to engage in strenuous physical activity, lameness, and pain may be (though not always) signs of hip dysplasia, usually manifested between the ages of 4 months and 1 year. Climbing stairs or rising from a sitting or lying position may be difficult, and the dog may cry out if the hip joint is manipulated. Your veterinarian can help differentiate these symptoms of hip dysplasia from similar symptoms relating to skeletal growth abnormalities, such as osteodystrophy.

Hip dysplasia can cause a wide range of problems, from mild lameness to movement irregularities to crippling pain. Dogs with hip dysplasia must often limit their activities, may need corrective surgery, or may even need to be euthanized because of the pain.

Hip dysplasia is considered to be a polygenic inherited disorder, which means many different genes may lead to the disease. Also, environmental factors may contribute to the development of hip dysplasia, including nutrition and exercise, although the part environmental factors play in the disease is highly debated among experts.

Special X-rays that show evidence of abnormal joint laxity are used to diagnose the condition. Once the X-ray is taken, it can be sent to the Orthopedic

Your dog needs sound hips to be the athlete she was born to be. That's why responsible breeders screen their dogs for hip dysplasia before breeding.

Foundation for Animals (OFA) which reads, grades, and certifies the X-rays of dogs over the age of 2 years. Sound hips are rated excellent, good, or fair, and the dog's owner receives a certificate with the rating. A dysplastic dog will be rated as mild, moderate, or severe. The University of Pennsylvania Hip Improvement Program (PennHIP) can evaluate hips as early as 16 weeks of age. Any dog who is found to be dysplastic should be removed from any breeding program.

Hypothyroidism

Hypothyroidism—in which the thyroid gland does not produce enough hormone—is becoming all too common in adult Boxers. Hypothyroidism may be caused by thyroid tumors or a primary malfunction of the gland. The deficient thyroid may affect many organ systems, including the heart.

Signs may include excessive hair thinning and loss, obesity, anemia, reproductive failures and infertility, and lethargy. The diagnosis is confirmed with a full panel of specific thyroid blood tests. Carefully determined doses of replacement hormone will alleviate most symptoms and will probably need to be given for the rest of the dog's life.

The Aging Boxer

Canine geriatric medicine has made great advances over the past several years. Full and happy lives can often be prolonged with appropriate medical treatments designed to rejuvenate and relieve the stress from failing organ systems. The elder Boxer is a great gift—a treasured friend who has shared and enriched your family members' lives for many years.

Age-Related Changes

While most Boxers tend to act youthful all their lives, your elder statesman may decline to run and play as she once did. She may develop arthritis; if she suffered any skeletal or joint injuries in her life, they may begin to cause her discomfort. She may have difficulty rising or exhibit intermittent lameness. There are excellent pain remedies for these problems that can be prescribed by your veterinarian.

Your own responsibilities to the geriatric dog are mostly a matter of common sense. She should not be allowed to become obese. Extra weight in dogs, as in people, puts undue stress on the heart and skeletal system. As your Boxer ages, her metabolism will slow and she will require fewer calories. There are excellent foods that are carefully formulated for older dogs.

If your Boxer seems inclined to tear around as if she were a puppy, but you know that she has a fragile knee joint or spinal arthritis or a bad heart, limit her exercise within sensible parameters. Give her a nice soft bed to lie on. And above all, keep up her grooming, keep her toenails trimmed, and make her feel that she is still a valued member of the family.

Saying Good-Bye

When the time comes to say good-bye, you may be lucky enough to find your old friend has left you as if she were dreaming on her favorite corner of the rug. Or you may have to make the most painful of decisions: to end your Boxer's incurable suffering in the most humane way possible, via veterinary euthanasia.

Euthanasia is, simply, an overdose of anesthesia. The dog will peacefully go to sleep before the overdose causes her heart to stop. If you make this difficult choice (and it is wrenching), steel yourself and remain with your dog while the procedure is being performed. Remember—your Boxer does not know what is happening, and the last thing you want her to hear is the soothing sound of your voice as she drifts asleep. You owe her no less. It has been a remarkable journey.

Part III
Enjoying
Your Boxer

Chapter 9

Training Your Boxer

by Peggy Moran

Training makes your best friend better! A properly trained dog has a happier life and a longer life expectancy. He is also more appreciated by the people he encounters each day, both at home and out and about.

A trained dog walks nicely and joins his family often, going places untrained dogs cannot go. He is never rude or unruly, and he always happily comes when called. When he meets people for the first time, he greets them by sitting and waiting to be petted, rather than jumping up. At home he doesn't compete with his human family, and alone he is not destructive or overly anxious. He isn't continually nagged with words like "no," since he has learned not to misbehave in the first place. He is never shamed, harshly punished, or treated unkindly, and he is a well-loved, involved member of the family.

Sounds good, doesn't it? If you are willing to invest some time, thought, and patience, the words above could soon be used to describe your dog (though perhaps changing "he" to "she"). Educating your pet in a positive way is fun and easy, and there is no better gift you can give your pet than the guarantee of improved understanding and a great relationship.

This chapter will explain how to offer kind leadership, reshape your pet's behavior in a positive and practical way, and even get a head start on simple obedience training.

Understanding Builds the Bond

Dog training is a learning adventure on both ends of the leash. Before attempting to teach their dog new behaviors or change unwanted ones, thoughtful dog owners take the time to understand why their pets behave the way they do, and how their own behavior can be either a positive or negative influence on their dog.

Canine Nature

Loving dogs as much as we do, it's easy to forget they are a completely different species. Despite sharing our homes and living as appreciated members of our families, dogs do not think or learn exactly the same way people do. Even if you love your dog like a child, you must remember to respect the fact that he is actually a dog.

Dogs have no idea when their behavior is inappropriate from a human perspective. They are not aware of the value of possessions they chew or of messes they make or the worry they sometimes seem to cause. While people tend to look at behavior as good and bad or right and wrong, dogs just discover what works and what doesn't work. Then they behave accordingly, learning from their own experiences and increasing or reducing behaviors to improve results for themselves.

You might wonder, "But don't dogs want to please us"? My answer is yes, provided your pleasure reflects back to them in positive ways they can feel and appreciate. Dogs do things for *dog* reasons, and everything they do works for them in some way or they wouldn't be doing it!

The Social Dog

Our pets descended from animals who lived in tightly knit, cooperative social groups. Though far removed in appearance and lifestyle from their ancestors, our dogs still relate in many of the same ways their wild relatives did. And in their relationships with one another, wild canids either lead or follow.

Canine ranking relationships are not about cruelty and power; they are about achievement and abilities. Competent dogs with high levels of drive and confidence step up, while deferring dogs step aside. But followers don't get the short end of the stick; they benefit from the security of having a more competent dog at the helm.

Our domestic dogs still measure themselves against other members of their group—us! Dog owners whose actions lead to positive results have willing, secure followers. But dogs may step up and fill the void or cut loose and do their own thing when their people fail to show capable leadership. When dogs are pushy, aggressive, and rude, or independent and unwilling, it's not because they have designs on the role of "master." It is more likely their owners failed to provide consistent leadership.

Dogs in training benefit from their handler's good leadership. Their education flows smoothly because they are impressed. Being in charge doesn't require you to physically dominate or punish your dog. You simply need to make some subtle changes in the way you relate to him every day.

Lead Your Pack!

Create schedules and structure daily activities. Dogs are creatures of habit and routines will create security. Feed meals at the same times each day and also try to schedule regular walks, training practices, and toilet outings. Your predictability will help your dog be patient.

Ask your dog to perform a task. Before releasing him to food or freedom, have him do something as simple as sit on command. Teach him that cooperation earns great results!

Give a release prompt (such as "let's go") when going through doors leading outside. This is a better idea than allowing your impatient pup to rush past you.

Pet your dog when he is calm, not when he is excited. Turn your touch into a tool that relaxes and settles.

Reward desirable rather than inappropriate behavior. Petting a jumping dog (who hasn't been invited up) reinforces jumping. Pet sitting dogs, and only invite lap dogs up after they've first "asked" by waiting for your invitation.

Replace personal punishment with positive reinforcement. Show a dog what *to do,* and motivate him to want to do it, and there will be no need to punish him for what he should *not do.* Dogs naturally follow, without the need for force or harshness.

Play creatively and appropriately. Your dog will learn the most about his social rank when he is playing with you. During play, dogs work to control toys and try to get the best of one another in a friendly way. The wrong sorts of play can create problems: For example, tug of war can lead to aggressiveness. Allowing your dog to control toys during play may result in possessive guarding when he has something he really values, such as a bone. Dogs who are chased during play may later run away from you when you approach to leash them. The right kinds of play will help increase your dog's social confidence while you gently assert your leadership.

How Dogs Learn (and How They Don't)

Dog training begins as a meeting of minds—yours and your dog's. Though the end goal may be to get your dog's body to behave in a specific way, training starts as a mind game. Your dog is learning all the time by observing the consequences of his actions and social interactions. He is always seeking out what he perceives as desirable and trying to avoid what he perceives as undesirable.

He will naturally repeat a behavior that either brings him more good stuff or makes bad stuff go away (these are both types of reinforcement). He will naturally avoid a behavior that brings him more bad stuff or makes the good stuff go away (these are both types of punishment).

Both reinforcement and punishment can be perceived as either the direct result of something the dog did himself, or as coming from an outside source.

Using Life's Rewards

Your best friend is smart and he is also cooperative. When the best things in life can only be had by working with you, your dog will view you as a facilitator. You unlock doors to all of the positively reinforcing experiences he values: his freedom, his friends at the park, food, affection, walks, and play. The trained dog accompanies you through those doors and waits to see what working with you will bring.

Rewarding your dog for good behavior is called positive reinforcement, and, as we've just seen, it increases the likelihood that he will repeat that behavior. The perfect reward is anything your dog wants that is safe and appropriate. Don't limit yourself to toys, treats, and things that come directly from you. Harness life's positives—barking at squirrels, chasing a falling leaf, bounding away from you at the dog park, pausing for a moment to sniff everything—and allow your dog to earn access to those things as rewards that come from cooperating with you. When he looks at you, when he sits, when he comes when you call—any prompted behavior can earn one of life's rewards. When he works with you, he earns the things he most appreciates; but when he tries to get those things on his own, he cannot. Rather than seeing you as someone who always says "no," your dog will view you as the one who says "let's go!" He will *want* to follow.

What About Punishment?

Not only is it unnecessary to personally punish dogs, it is abusive. No matter how convinced you are that your dog "knows right from wrong," in reality he will associate personal punishment with the punisher. The resulting cowering, "guilty"-looking postures are actually displays of submission and fear. Later,

Purely Positive Reinforcement

With positive training, we emphasize teaching dogs what they should do to earn reinforcements, rather than punishing them for unwanted behaviors.

- Focus on teaching "do" rather than "don't." For example, a sitting dog isn't jumping.
- Use positive reinforcers that are valuable to your dog and the situation: A tired dog values rest; a confined dog values freedom.
- Play (appropriately)!
- Be a consistent leader.
- Set your dog up for success by anticipating and preventing problems.
- Notice and reward desirable behavior, and give him lots of attention when he is being good.
- Train ethically. Use humane methods and equipment that do not frighten or hurt your dog.
- When you are angry, walk away and plan a positive strategy.
- Keep practice sessions short and sweet. Five to ten minutes, three to five times a day is best.

when the punisher isn't around and the coast is clear, the same behavior he was punished for—such as raiding a trash can—might bring a self-delivered, very tasty result. The punished dog hasn't learned not to misbehave; he has learned to not get caught.

Does punishment ever have a place in dog training? Many people will heartily insist it does not. But dog owners often get frustrated as they try to stick to the path of all-positive reinforcement. It sure sounds great, but is it realistic, or even natural, to *never* say "no" to your dog?

A wild dog's life is not *all* positive. Hunger and thirst are both examples of negative reinforcement; the resulting discomfort motivates the wild dog to seek food and water. He encounters natural aversives such as pesky insects; mats in his coat; cold days; rainy days; sweltering hot days; and occasional run-ins with thorns, brambles, skunks, bees, and other nastiness. These all affect his behavior, as he tries to avoid the bad stuff whenever possible. The wild dog also occasionally encounters social punishers from others in his group when he gets too pushy. Starting with a growl or a snap from Mom, and later some mild and ritualized discipline from other members of his four-legged family, he learns to modify behaviors that elicit grouchy responses.

Our pet dogs don't naturally experience all positive results either, because they learn from their surroundings and from social experiences with other dogs. Watch a group of pet dogs playing together and you'll see a very old educational system still being used. As they wrestle and attempt to assert themselves, you'll notice many mouth-on-neck moments. Their playful biting is inhibited, with no intention to cause harm, but their message is clear: "Say uncle or this could hurt more!"

Observing that punishment does occur in nature, some people may feel compelled to try to be like the big wolf with their pet dogs. Becoming aggressive or heavy-handed with your pet will backfire! Your dog will not be impressed, nor will he want to follow you. Punishment causes dogs to change their behavior to avoid or escape discomfort and threats. Threatened dogs will either become very passive and offer submissive, appeasing postures, attempt to flee, or rise to the occasion and fight back. When people personally punish their dogs in an angry manner, one of these three defensive mechanisms will be triggered. Which one depends on a dog's genetic temperament as well as his past social experiences. Since we don't want to make our pets feel the need to avoid or escape us, personal punishment has no place in our training.

Remote Consequences

Sometimes, however, all-positive reinforcement is just not enough. That's because not all reinforcement comes from us. An inappropriate behavior can be self-reinforcing—just doing it makes the dog feel better in some way, whether you are there to say "good boy!" or not. Some examples are eating garbage, pulling the stuffing out of your sofa, barking at passersby, or urinating on the floor.

Although you don't want to personally punish your dog, the occasional deterrent may be called for to help derail these kinds of self-rewarding misbehaviors. In these cases, mild forms of impersonal or remote punishment can be used as part of a correction. The goal isn't to make your dog feel bad or to "know he has done wrong," but to help redirect him to alternate behaviors that are more acceptable to you.

The Problems with Personal Punishment

- Personally punished dogs are not taught appropriate behaviors.
- Personally punished dogs only stop misbehaving when they are caught or interrupted, but they don't learn not to misbehave when they are alone.
- Personally punished dogs become shy, fearful, and distrusting.
- Personally punished dogs may become defensively aggressive.
- Personally punished dogs become suppressed and inhibited.
- Personally punished dogs become stressed, triggering stress-reducing behaviors that their owners interpret as acts of spite, triggering even more punishment.
- Personally punished dogs have stressed owners.
- Personally punished dogs may begin to repeat behaviors they have been taught will result in negative, but predictable, attention.
- Personally punished dogs are more likely to be given away than are positively trained dogs.

You do this by pairing a slightly startling, totally impersonal sound with an equally impersonal and *very mild* remote consequence. The impersonal sound might be a single shake of an empty plastic pop bottle with pennies in it, held out of your dog's sight. Or you could use a vocal expression such as "eh!" delivered with you looking *away* from your misbehaving dog.

Pair your chosen sound—the penny bottle or "eh!"—with either a slight tug on his collar or a sneaky spritz on the rump from a water bottle. Do this right *as* he touches something he should not; bad timing will confuse your dog and undermine your training success.

To keep things under your control and make sure you get the timing right, it's best to do this as a setup. "Accidentally" drop a shoe on the floor, and then help your dog learn some things are best avoided. As he sniffs the shoe say "eh!" without looking at him and give a *slight* tug against his collar. This sound will quickly become meaningful as a correction all by itself—sometimes after just one setup—making the tug correction obsolete. The tug lets your dog see that you were right; going for that shoe *was* a bad idea! Your wise dog will be more likely to heed your warning next time, and probably move closer to you where it's safe. Be a good friend and pick up the nasty shoe. He'll be relieved and you'll look heroic. Later, when he's home alone and encounters a stray shoe, he'll want to give it a wide berth.

Your negative marking sound will come in handy in the future, when your dog begins to venture down the wrong behavioral path. The goal is not to announce your disapproval or to threaten your dog. You are not telling him to stop or showing how *you* feel about his behavior. You are sounding a warning to a friend who's venturing off toward danger—"I wouldn't if I were you!" Suddenly, there is an abrupt, rather startling, noise! Now is the moment to redirect him and help him earn positive reinforcement. That interrupted behavior will become something he wants to avoid in the future, but he won't want to avoid you.

Practical Commands for Family Pets

Before you begin training your dog, let's look at some equipment you'll want to have on hand:

- **A buckle collar** is fine for most dogs. If your dog pulls *very* hard, try a head collar, a device similar to a horse halter that helps reduce pulling by turning the dog's head. *Do not* use a choke chain (sometimes called a training collar), because they cause physical harm even when used correctly.
- **Six-foot training leash and twenty-six–foot retractable leash.**
- **A few empty plastic soda bottles with about twenty pennies in each one.** This will be used to impersonally interrupt misbehaviors before redirecting dogs to more positive activities.
- **A favorite squeaky toy,** to motivate, attract attention, and reward your dog during training.

Lure your dog to take just a few steps with you on the leash by being inviting and enthusiastic. Make sure you reward him for his efforts.

Baby Steps

Allow your young pup to drag a short, lightweight leash attached to a buckle collar for a few *supervised* moments, several times each day. At first the leash may annoy him and he may jump around a bit trying to get away from it. Distract him with your squeaky toy or a bit of his kibble and he'll quickly get used to his new "tail."

Begin walking him on the leash by holding the end and following him. As he adapts, you can begin to assert gentle direct pressure to teach him to follow you. Don't jerk or yank, or he will become afraid to walk when the leash is on. If he becomes hesitant, squat down facing him and let him figure out that by moving toward you he is safe and secure. If he remains confused or frightened and doesn't come to you, go to him and help him understand that you provide safe harbor while he's on the leash. Then back away a few steps and try again to lure him to you. As he learns that you are the "home base," he'll want to follow when you walk a few steps, waiting for you to stop, squat down, and make him feel great.

So Attached to You!

The next step in training your dog—and this is a very important one—is to begin spending at least an hour or more each day with him on a four- to six-foot leash, held by or tethered to you. This training will increase his attachment to you—literally!—as you sit quietly or walk about, tending to your household business. When you are quiet, he'll learn it is time to settle; when you are active, he'll learn to move with you. Tethering also keeps him out of trouble when you are busy but still want his company. It is a great alternative to confining a dog, and can be used instead of crating any time you're home and need to slow him down a bit.

Rotating your dog from supervised freedom to tethered time to some quiet time in the crate or his gated area gives him a diverse and balanced day while he is learning. Two confined or tethered hours is the most you should require of your dog in one stretch, before changing to some supervised freedom, play, or a walk.

The dog in training may, at times, be stressed by all of the changes he is dealing with. Provide a stress outlet, such as a toy to chew on, when he is confined or tethered. He will settle into his quiet time more quickly and completely. Always be sure to provide several rounds of daily play and free time (in a fenced area or on your retractable leash) in addition to plenty of chewing materials.

Dog Talk

Dogs don't speak in words, but they do have a language—body language. They use postures, vocalizations, movements, facial gestures,

Tethering your dog is a great way to keep him calm and under control, but still with you.

odors, and touch—usually with their mouths—to communicate what they are feeling and thinking.

We also "speak" using body language. We have quite an array of postures, movements, and facial gestures that accompany our touch and language as we attempt to communicate with our pets. And our dogs can quickly figure us out!

Alone, without associations, words are just noises. But, because we pair them with meaningful body language, our dogs make the connection. Dogs can really learn to understand much of what we *say*, if what we *do* at the same time is consistent.

The Positive Marker

Start your dog's education with one of the best tricks in dog training: Pair various positive reinforcers—food, a toy, touch—with a sound such as a click on a clicker (which you can get at the pet supply store) or a spoken word like "good!" or "yes!" This will enable you to later "mark" your dog's desirable behaviors.

It seems too easy: Just say "yes!" and give the dog his toy. (Or use whatever sound and reward you have chosen.) Later, when you make your marking sound right at the instant your dog does the right thing, he will know you are going to be giving him something good for that particular action. And he'll be eager to repeat the behavior to hear you mark it again!

Next, you must teach your dog to understand the meaning of cues you'll be using to ask him to perform specific behaviors. This is easy, too. Does he already do things you might like him to do on command? Of course! He lies down, he sits, he picks things up, he drops them again, he comes to you. All of the behaviors you'd like to control are already part of your dog's natural repertoire. The trick is getting him to offer those behaviors when you ask for them. And that means you have to teach him to associate a particular behavior on his part with a particular behavior on your part.

Sit Happens

Teach your dog an important new rule: From now on, he is only touched and petted when he is either sitting or lying down. You won't need to ask him to sit; in fact, you should not. Just keeping him tethered near you so there isn't much to do but stand, be ignored, or settle, and wait until sit happens.

He may pester you a bit, but be stoic and unresponsive. Starting now, when *you* are sitting down, a sitting dog is the only one you see and pay attention to. He will eventually sit, and as he does, attach the word "sit"—but don't be too excited or he'll jump right back up. Now mark with your positive sound that promises something good, then reward him with a slow, quiet, settling pet.

Training requires consistent reinforcement. Ask others to also wait until your dog is sitting and calm to touch him, and he will associate being petted with being relaxed. Be sure you train your dog to associate everyone's touch with quiet bonding.

Reinforcing "Sit" as a Command

Since your dog now understands one concept of working for a living—sit to earn petting—you can begin to shape and reinforce his desire to sit. Hold toys, treats, his bowl of food, and turn into a statue. But don't prompt him to sit! Instead, remain frozen and unavailable, looking somewhere out into space, over his head. He will put on a bit of a show, trying to get a response from you, and may offer various behaviors, but only one will push your button—sitting. Wait for him to offer the "right" behavior, and when he does, you unfreeze. Say "sit," then mark with an excited "good!" and give him the toy or treat with a release command—"OK!"

When you notice spontaneous sits occurring, be sure to take advantage of those free opportunities to make your command sequence meaningful and positive. Say "sit" as you observe sit happen—then mark with "good!" and praise, pet, or reward the dog. Soon, every time you look at your dog he'll be sitting and looking right back at you!

Now, after thirty days of purely positive practice, it's time to give him a test. When he is just walking around doing his own thing, suddenly ask him to sit. He'll probably do it right away. If he doesn't, do *not* repeat your command, or you'll just undermine its meaning ("sit" means sit *now;* the command is not "sit, sit, sit, sit"). Instead, get something he likes and let him know you have it. Wait for him to offer the sit—he will—then say "sit!" and complete your marking and rewarding sequence.

OK

"OK" will probably rate as one of your dog's favorite words. It's like the word "recess" to schoolchildren. It is the word used to release your dog from a command. You can introduce "OK" during your "sit" practice. When he gets up from a sit, say "OK" to tell him the sitting is finished. Soon that sound will mean "freedom."

Make it even more meaningful and positive. Whenever he spontaneously bounds away, say "OK!" Squeak a toy, and when he notices and shows interest, toss it for him.

Down

I've mentioned that you should only pet your dog when he is either sitting or lying down. Now, using the approach I've just introduced for "sit," teach your dog to lie down. You will be a statue, and hold something he would like to get but that you'll only release to a dog who is lying down. It helps to lower the desired item to the floor in front of him, still not speaking and not letting him have it until he offers you the new behavior you are seeking.

Lower your dog's reward to the floor to help him figure out what behavior will earn him his reward.

He may offer a sit and then wait expectantly, but you must make him keep searching for the new trick that triggers your generosity. Allow your dog to experiment and find the right answer, even if he has to search around for it first. When he lands on "down" and learns it is another behavior that works, he'll offer it more quickly the next time.

Don't say "down" until he lies down, to tightly associate your prompt with the correct behavior. To say "down, down, down" as he is sitting, looking at you, or pawing at the toy would make "down" mean those behaviors instead! Whichever behavior he offers, a training opportunity has been created. Once you've attached and shaped both sitting and lying down, you can ask for both behaviors with your verbal prompts, "sit" or "down." Be sure to only reinforce the "correct" reply!

Stay

"Stay" can easily be taught as an extension of what you've already been practicing. To teach "stay," you follow the entire sequence for reinforcing a "sit" or "down," except you wait a bit longer before you give the release word, "OK!" Wait a second or two longer during each practice before saying "OK!" and releasing your dog to the positive reinforcer (toy, treat, or one of life's other rewards).

You can step on the leash to help your dog understand the down-stay, but only do this when he is already lying down. You don't want to hurt him!

If he gets up before you've said "OK," you have two choices: pretend the release was your idea and quickly interject "OK!" as he breaks; or, if he is more experienced and practiced, mark the behavior with your correction sound—"eh!"— and then gently put him back on the spot, wait for him to lie down, and begin again. Be sure the next three practices are a success. Ask him to wait for just a second, and release him before he can be wrong. You need to keep your dog feeling like more of a success than a failure as you begin to test his training in increasingly more distracting and difficult situations.

As he gets the hang of it—he stays until you say "OK"— you can gradually push for longer times—up to a minute on a sit-stay, and up to three minutes on a down-stay. You can also gradually add distractions and work in new environments. To add a minor self-correction for the down-stay, stand on the dog's leash after he lies down, allowing about three inches of slack. If tries to get up before you've said "OK," he'll discover it doesn't work.

Do not step on the leash to make your dog lie down! This could badly hurt his neck, and will destroy his trust in you. Remember, we are teaching our dogs to make the best choices, not inflicting our answers upon them!

Come

Rather than thinking of "come" as an action—"come to me"—think of it as a place—"the dog is sitting in front of me, facing me." Since your dog by now really likes sitting to earn your touch and other positive reinforcement, he's likely to sometimes sit directly in front of you, facing you, all on his own. When this happens, give it a specific name: "come."

Now follow the rest of the training steps you have learned to make him like doing it and reinforce the behavior by practicing it any chance you get. Anything your dog wants and likes could be earned as a result of his first offering the sit-in-front known as "come."

You can help guide him into the right location. Use your hands as "landing gear" and pat the insides of your legs at his nose level. Do this while backing up a bit, to help him maneuver to the straight-in-front, facing-you position. Don't say the

Pat the insides of your legs to show your dog exactly where you like him to sit when you say "come."

word "come" while he's maneuvering, because he hasn't! You are trying to make "come" the end result, not the work in progress.

You can also help your dog by marking his movement in the right direction: Use your positive sound or word to promise he is getting warm. When he finally sits facing you, enthusiastically say "come," mark again with your positive word, and release him with an enthusiastic "OK!" Make it so worth his while, with lots of play and praise, that he can't wait for you to ask him to come again!

Building a Better Recall

Practice, practice, practice. Now, practice some more. Teach your dog that all good things in life hinge upon him first sitting in front of you in a behavior named "come." When you think he really has got it, test him by asking him to "come" as you gradually add distractions and change locations. Expect setbacks as you make these changes and practice accordingly. Lower your expectations and make his task easier so he is able to get it right. Use those distractions as rewards, when they are appropriate. For example, let him check out the interesting leaf that blew by as a reward for first coming to you and ignoring it.

Add distance and call your dog to come while he is on his retractable leash. If he refuses and sits looking at you blankly, *do not* jerk, tug, "pop," or reel him in. Do nothing! It is his move; wait to see what behavior he offers. He'll either begin to approach (mark the behavior with an excited "good!"), sit and do nothing (just keep waiting), or he'll try to move in some direction other than toward you. If he tries to leave, use your correction marker—"eh!"— and bring him to a stop by letting him walk to the end of the leash, *not* by jerking him. Now walk to him in a neutral manner, and don't jerk or show any disapproval. Gently bring him back to the spot where he was when you called him, then back away and face him, still waiting and not reissuing your command. Let him keep examining his options until he finds the one that works—yours!

If you have practiced everything I've suggested so far and given your dog a chance to really learn what "come" means, he is well aware of what you want and is quite intelligently weighing all his options. The only way he'll know your way is the one that works is to be allowed to examine his other choices and discover that they *don't* work.

Sooner or later every dog tests his training. Don't be offended or angry when your dog tests you. No matter how positive you've made it, he won't always want to do everything you ask, every time. When he explores the "what happens if I don't" scenario, your training is being strengthened. He will discover through his own process of trial and error that the best—and only—way out of a command he really doesn't feel compelled to obey is to obey it.

Let's Go

Many pet owners wonder if they can retain control while walking their dogs and still allow at least some running in front, sniffing, and playing. You might worry that allowing your dog occasional freedom could result in him expecting it all the time, leading to a testy, leash-straining walk. It's possible for both parties on the leash to have an enjoyable experience by implementing and reinforcing well-thought-out training techniques.

Begin by making word associations you'll use on your walks. Give the dog some slack on the leash, and as he starts to walk away from you say "OK" and begin to follow him.

Give your dog slack on his leash as you walk and let him make the decision to walk with you.

Do not let him drag you; set the pace even when he is being given a turn at being the leader. Whenever he starts to pull, just come to a standstill and refuse to move (or refuse to allow him to continue forward) until there is slack in the leash. Do this correction without saying anything at all. When he isn't pulling, you may decide to just stand still and let him sniff about within the range the slack leash allows, or you may even mosey along following him. After a few minutes of "recess," it is time to work. Say something like "that's it" or "time's up," close the distance between you and your dog, and touch him.

Next say "let's go" (or whatever command you want to use to mean "follow me as we walk"). Turn and walk off, and, if he follows, mark his behavior with "good!" Then stop,

When your dog catches up with you, make sure you let him know what a great dog he is!

Intersperse periods of attentive walking, where your dog is on a shorter leash, with periods on a slack leash, where he is allowed to look and sniff around.

squat down, and let him catch you. Make him glad he did! Start again, and do a few transitions as he gets the hang of your follow-the-leader game, speeding up, slowing down, and trying to make it fun. When you stop, he gets to catch up and receive some deserved positive reinforcement. Don't forget that's the reason he is following you, so be sure to make it worth his while!

Require him to remain attentive to you. Do not allow sniffing, playing, eliminating, or pulling during your time as leader on a walk. If he seems to get distracted—which, by the way, is the main reason dogs walk poorly with their people—change direction or pace without saying a word. Just help him realize "oops, I lost track of my human." Do not jerk his neck and say "heel"—this will make the word "heel" mean pain in the neck and will not encourage him to cooperate with you. Don't repeat "let's go," either. He needs to figure out that it is his job to keep track of and follow you if he wants to earn the positive benefits you provide.

The best reward you can give a dog for performing an attentive, controlled walk is a few minutes of walking without all of the controls. Of course, he must remain on a leash even during the "recess" parts of the walk, but allowing him to discriminate between attentive following—"let's go"—and having a few moments of relaxation—"OK"—will increase his willingness to work.

Training for Attention

Your dog pretty much has a one-track mind. Once he is focused on something, everything else is excluded. This can be great, for instance, when he's focusing on you! But it can also be dangerous if, for example, his attention is riveted on the bunny he is chasing and he does not hear you call—that is, not unless he has been trained to pay attention when you say his name.

When you say your dog's name, you'll want him to make eye contact with you. Begin teaching this by making yourself so intriguing that he can't help but look.

When you call your dog's name, you will again be seeking a specific response—eye contact. The best way to teach this is to trigger his alerting response by making a noise with your mouth, such as whistling or a kissing sound, and then immediately doing something he'll find very intriguing.

You can play a treasure hunt game to help teach him to regard his name as a request for attention. As a bonus, you can reinforce the rest of his new vocabulary at the same time.

Treasure Hunt

Make a kissing sound, then jump up and find a dog toy or dramatically raid the fridge and rather noisily eat a piece of cheese. After doing this twice, make a kissing sound and then look at your dog.

Of course he is looking at you! He is waiting to see if that sound—the kissing sound—means you're going to go hunting again. After all, you're so good at it! Because he is looking, say his name, mark with "good," then go hunting and find his toy. Release it to him with an "OK." At any point if he follows you, attach your "let's go!" command; if he leaves you, give permission with "OK."

Using this approach, he cannot be wrong—any behavior your dog offers can be named. You can add things like "take it" when he picks up a toy, and "thank you" when he happens to drop one. Many opportunities to make your new vocabulary meaningful and positive can be found within this simple training game.

Problems to watch out for when teaching the treasure hunt:

- You really do not want your dog to come to you when you call his name (later, when you try to engage his attention to ask him to stay, he'll already be on his way toward you). You just want him to look at you.
- Saying "watch me, watch me" doesn't teach your dog to *offer* his attention. It just makes you a background noise.
- Don't lure your dog's attention with the reward. Get his attention and then reward him for looking. Try holding a toy in one hand with your arm stretched out to your side. Wait until he looks at you rather than the toy. Now say his name then mark with "good!" and release the toy. As he goes for it, say "OK."

To get your dog's attention, try holding his toy with your arm out to your side. Wait until he looks at you, then mark the moment and give him the toy.

Teaching Cooperation

Never punish your dog for failing to obey you or try to punish him into compliance. Bribing, repeating yourself, and doing a behavior for him all avoid the real issue of dog training—his will. He must be helped to be willing, not made to achieve tasks. Good dog training helps your dog want to obey. He learns that he can gain what he values most through cooperation and compliance, and can't gain those things any other way.

Your dog is learning to *earn,* rather than expect, the good things in life. And you've become much more important to him than you were before. Because you are allowing him to experiment and learn, he doesn't have to be forced, manipulated, or bribed. When he wants something, he can gain it by cooperating with you. One of those "somethings"—and a great reward you shouldn't underestimate—is your positive attention, paid to him with love and sincere approval!

Chapter 10

Housetraining Your Boxer

Excerpted from Housetraining: An Owner's Guide to a Happy Healthy Pet, 1st Edition, *by September Morn*

By the time puppies are about 3 weeks old, they start to follow their mother around. When they are a few steps away from their clean sleeping area, the mama dog stops. The pups try to nurse but mom won't allow it. The pups mill around in frustration, then nature calls and they all urinate and defecate here, away from their bed. The mother dog returns to the nest, with her brood waddling behind her. Their first housetraining lesson has been a success.

The next one to housetrain puppies should be their breeder. The breeder watches as the puppies eliminate, then deftly removes the soiled papers and replaces them with clean papers before the pups can traipse back through their messes. He has wisely arranged the puppies' space so their bed, food, and drinking water are as far away from the elimination area as possible. This way, when the pups follow their mama, they will move away from their sleeping and eating area before eliminating. This habit will help the pups be easily housetrained.

Your Housetraining Shopping List

While your puppy's mother and breeder are getting her started on good house-training habits, you'll need to do some shopping. If you have all the essentials in place before your dog arrives, it will be easier to help her learn the rules from day one.

Newspaper: The younger your puppy and larger her breed, the more newspapers you'll need. Newspaper is absorbent, abundant, cheap, and convenient.

Puddle Pads: If you prefer not to stockpile newspaper, a commercial alternative is puddle pads. These thick paper pads can be purchased under several trade names at pet supply stores. The pads have waterproof backing, so puppy urine doesn't seep through onto the floor. Their disadvantages are that they will cost you more than newspapers and that they contain plastics that are not biodegradable.

Poop Removal Tool: There are several types of poop removal tools available. Some are designed with a separate pan and rake, and others have the handles hinged like scissors. Some scoops need two hands for operation, while others are designed for one-handed use. Try out the different brands at your pet supply store. Put a handful of pebbles or dog kibble on the floor and then pick them up with each type of scoop to determine which works best for you.

Plastic Bags: When you take your dog outside your yard, you *must* pick up after her. Dog waste is unsightly, smelly, and can harbor disease. In many cities and towns, the law mandates dog owners clean up pet waste deposited on public ground. Picking up after your dog using a plastic bag scoop is simple. Just put your hand inside the bag, like a mitten, and then grab the droppings. Turn the bag inside out, tie the top, and that's that.

Crate: To housetrain a puppy, you will need some way to confine her when you're unable to supervise. A dog crate is a secure way to confine your dog for short periods during the day and to use as a comfortable bed at night. Crates come in wire mesh and in plastic. The wire ones are foldable to store flat in a smaller space. The plastic ones are more cozy, draft-free, and quiet, and are approved for airline travel.

Take your pup out frequently to her special potty spot and praise her when she goes.

Baby Gates: Since you shouldn't crate a dog for more than an hour or two at a time during the day, baby gates are a good way to limit your dog's freedom in the house. Be sure the baby gates you use are safe. The old-fashioned wooden, expanding lattice type has seriously injured a number of children by collapsing and trapping a leg, arm, or neck. That type of gate can hurt a puppy, too, so use the modern grid type gates instead. You'll need more than one baby gate if you have several doorways to close off.

Exercise Pen: Portable exercise pens are great when you have a young pup or a small dog. These metal or plastic pens are made of rectangular panels that are hinged together. The pens are freestanding, sturdy, foldable, and can be carried like a suitcase. You could set one up in your kitchen as the pup's daytime corral, and then take it outdoors to contain your pup while you garden or just sit and enjoy the day.

Enzymatic Cleaner: All dogs make housetraining mistakes. Accept this and be ready for it by buying an enzymatic cleaner made especially for pet accidents. Dogs like to eliminate where they have done it before, and lingering smells lead them to those spots. Ordinary household cleaners may remove all the odors you can smell, but only an enzymatic cleaner will remove everything your dog can smell.

The First Day

Housetraining is a matter of establishing good habits in your dog. That means you never want her to learn anything she will eventually have to unlearn. Start off housetraining on the right foot by teaching your dog that you prefer her to eliminate outside. Designate a potty area in your backyard (if you have one) or in the street in front of your home and take your dog to it as soon as you arrive home. Let her sniff a bit and, when she squats to go, give the action a name: "potty" or "do it" or anything else you won't be embarrassed to say in public.

Eventually your dog will associate that word with the act and will eliminate on command. When she's finished, praise her with "good potty!"

That first day, take your puppy out to the potty area frequently. Although she may not eliminate every time, you are establishing a routine: You take her to her spot, ask her to eliminate, and praise her when she does.

Just before bedtime, take your dog to her potty area once more. Stand by and wait until she produces. Do not put your dog to bed for the night until she has eliminated. Be patient and calm. This is not the time to play with or excite your dog. If she's too excited, a pup not only won't eliminate, she probably won't want to sleep either.

Most dogs, even young ones, will not soil their beds if they can avoid it. For this reason, a sleeping crate can be a tremendous help during housetraining.

Your dog's crate is a great housetraining tool.

Don't Overuse the Crate

A crate serves well as a dog's overnight bed, but you should not leave the dog in her crate for more than an hour or two during the day. Throughout the day, she needs to play and exercise. She is likely to want to drink some water and will undoubtedly eliminate. Confining your dog all day will give her no option but to soil her crate. This is not just unpleasant for you and the dog, but it reinforces bad cleanliness habits. And crating a pup for the whole day is abusive. Don't do it.

Being crated at night can help a dog develop the muscles that control elimination. So after your dog has emptied out, put her to bed in her crate.

A good place to put your dog's sleeping crate is near your own bed. Dogs are pack animals, so they feel safer sleeping with others in a common area. In your bedroom, the pup will be near you and you'll be close enough to hear when she wakes during the night and needs to eliminate.

Pups under 4 months old often are not able to hold their urine all night. If your puppy has settled down to sleep but awakens and fusses a few hours later, she probably needs to go out. For the best housetraining progress, take your pup to her elimination area whenever she needs to go, even in the wee hours of the morning.

Your pup may soil in her crate if you ignore her late night urgency. It's unfair to let this happen, and it sends the wrong message about your expectations for cleanliness. Resign yourself to this midnight outing and just get up and take the pup out. Your pup will outgrow this need soon and will learn in the process that she can count on you, and you'll wake happily each morning to a clean dog.

The next morning, the very first order of business is to take your pup out to eliminate. Don't forget to take her to her special potty spot, ask her to eliminate, and then praise her when she does. After your pup empties out in the morning, give her breakfast, and then take her to her potty area again. After that, she shouldn't need to eliminate again right away, so you can allow her some free playtime. Keep an eye on the pup though, because when she pauses in play she may need to go potty. Take her to the right spot, give the command, and praise if she produces.

Confine Your Pup

A pup or dog who has not finished housetraining should *never* be allowed the run of the house unattended. A new dog (especially a puppy) with unlimited access to your house will make her own choices about where to eliminate. Vigilance during your new dog's first few weeks in your home will pay big dividends. Every potty mistake delays housetraining progress; every success speeds it along.

Prevent problems by setting up a controlled environment for your new pet. A good place for a puppy corral is often the kitchen. Kitchens almost always have waterproof or easily cleaned floors, which is a distinct asset with leaky pups. A bathroom, laundry room, or enclosed porch could be used for a puppy corral, but the kitchen is generally the best location. Kitchens are a meeting place and a hub of activity for many families, and a puppy will learn better manners when she is socialized thoroughly with family, friends, and nice strangers.

The way you structure your pup's corral area is very important. Her bed, food, and water should be at the opposite end of the corral from the potty area. When you first get your pup, spread newspaper over the rest of the floor of her playpen corral. Lay the papers at least four pages thick and be sure to overlap the edges. As you note the pup's progress, you can remove the papers nearest the sleeping and eating corner. Gradually decrease the size of the papered area until only the end where you want the pup to eliminate is covered. If you will be training your dog to eliminate outside, place newspaper at the end of the corral that is closest to the door that leads outdoors. That way as she moves away from the clean area to the papered area, the pup will also form the habit of heading toward the door to go out.

Maintain a scent marker for the pup's potty area by reserving a small soiled piece of paper when you clean up. Place this piece, with her scent of urine, under the top sheet of the clean papers you spread. This will cue your pup where to eliminate.

Most dog owners use a combination of indoor papers and outdoor elimination areas. When the pup is

> ### T I P
>
> **Water**
>
> Make sure your dog has access to clean water at all times. Limiting the amount of water a dog drinks is not necessary for housetraining success and can be very dangerous. A dog needs water to digest food, to maintain a proper body temperature and proper blood volume, and to clean her system of toxins and wastes. A healthy dog will automatically drink the right amount. Do not restrict water intake. Controlling your dog's access to water is not the key to housetraining her; controlling her access to everything else in your home is.

left by herself in the corral, she can potty on the ever-present newspaper. When you are available to take the pup outside, she can do her business in the outdoor spot. It is not difficult to switch a pup from indoor paper training to outdoor elimination. Owners of large pups often switch early, but potty papers are still useful if the pup spends time in her indoor corral while you're away. Use the papers as long as your pup needs them. If you come home and they haven't been soiled, you are ahead.

When setting up your pup's outdoor yard, put the lounging area as far away as possible from the potty area, just as with the indoor corral setup. People with large yards, for example, might leave a patch unmowed at the edge of the lawn to serve as the dog's elimination area. Other dog owners teach the dog to relieve herself in a designated corner of a deck or patio. For an apartment-dwelling city dog, the outdoor potty area might be a tiny balcony or the curb. Each dog owner has somewhat different expectations for their dog. Teach your dog to eliminate in a spot that suits your environment and lifestyle.

Be sure to pick up droppings in your yard at least once a day. Dogs have a natural desire to stay far away from their own excrement, and if too many piles litter the ground, your dog won't want to walk through it and will start eliminating elsewhere. Leave just one small piece of feces in the potty area to remind your dog where the right spot is located.

To help a pup adapt to the change from indoors to outdoors, take one of her potty papers outside to the new elimination area. Let the pup stand on the paper

When you take your dog outside for a potty trip, don't play until after she's done. You don't want to distract her or confuse her about what this trip is for.

when she goes potty outdoors. Each day for four days, reduce the size of the paper by half. By the fifth day, the pup, having used a smaller and smaller piece of paper to stand on, will probably just go to that spot and eliminate.

Take your pup to her outdoor potty place frequently throughout the day. A puppy can hold her urine for only about as many hours as her age in months, and will move her bowels as many times a day as she eats. So a 2-month-old pup will urinate about every two hours, while at

When setting up your dog's outdoor space, put the area for play away from the potty area.

4 months she can manage about four hours between piddles. Pups vary somewhat in their rate of development, so this is not a hard and fast rule. It does, however, present a realistic idea of how long a pup can be left without access to a potty place. Past 4 months, her potty trips will be less frequent.

When you take the dog outdoors to her spot, keep her leashed so that she won't wander away. Stand quietly and let her sniff around in the designated area. If your pup starts to leave before she has eliminated, gently lead her back and remind her to go. If your pup sniffs at the spot, praise her calmly, say the command word, and just wait. If she produces, praise serenely, then give her time to sniff around a little more. She may not be finished, so give her time to go again before allowing her to play and explore her new home.

If you find yourself waiting more than five minutes for your dog to potty, take her back inside. Watch your pup carefully for twenty minutes, not giving her any opportunity to slip away to eliminate unnoticed. If you are too busy to watch the pup, put her in her crate. After twenty minutes, take her to the outdoor potty spot again and tell her what to do. If you're unsuccessful after five minutes, crate the dog again. Give her another chance to eliminate in fifteen or twenty minutes. Eventually, she will have to go.

Watch Your Pup

Be vigilant and don't let the pup make a mistake in the house. Each time you successfully anticipate elimination and take your pup to the potty spot, you'll move a step closer to your goal. Stay aware of your puppy's needs. If you ignore the pup, she will make mistakes and you'll be cleaning up more messes.

Housetraining is a huge task, but it doesn't go on forever. Be patient and soon your dog will be reliable.

Keep a chart of your new dog's elimination behavior for the first three or four days. Jot down what times she eats, sleeps, and eliminates. After several days a pattern will emerge that can help you determine your pup's body rhythms. Most dogs tend to eliminate at fairly regular intervals. Once you know your new dog's natural rhythms, you'll be able to anticipate her needs and schedule appropriate potty outings.

Understanding the meanings of your dog's postures can also help you win the battle of the puddle. When your dog is getting ready to eliminate, she will display a specific set of postures. The sooner you can learn to read these signals, the cleaner your floor will stay.

A young puppy who feels the urge to eliminate may start to sniff the ground and walk in a circle. If the pup is very young, she may simply squat and go. All young puppies, male or female, squat to urinate. If you are housetraining a pup under 4 months of age, regardless of sex, watch for the beginnings of a squat as the signal to rush the pup to the potty area.

When a puppy is getting ready to defecate, she may run urgently back and forth or turn in a circle while sniffing or starting to squat. If defecation is imminent, the pup's anus may protrude or open slightly. When she starts to go, the pup will squat and hunch her back, her tail sticking straight out behind. There is no mistaking this posture; nothing else looks like this. If your pup takes this position, take her to her potty area. Hurry! You may have to carry her to get there in time.

A young puppy won't have much time between feeling the urge and actually eliminating, so you'll have to be quick to note her postural clues and intercept your pup in time. Pups from 3 to 6 months have a few seconds more between the urge and the act than younger ones do. The older your pup, the more time you'll have to get her to the potty area after she begins the posture signals that alert you to her need.

Accidents Happen

If you see your pup about to eliminate somewhere other than the designated area, interrupt her immediately. Say "wait, wait, wait!" or clap your hands loudly to startle her into stopping. Carry the pup, if she's still small enough, or take her collar and lead her to the correct area. Once your dog is in the potty area, give her the command to eliminate. Use a friendly voice for the command, then wait patiently for her to produce. The pup may be tense because you've just startled her and may have to relax a bit before she's able to eliminate. When she does her job, include the command word in the praise you give ("good potty").

The old-fashioned way of housetraining involved punishing a dog's mistakes even before she knew what she was supposed to do. Puppies were punished for breaking rules they didn't understand about functions they couldn't control. This was not fair. While your dog is new to housetraining, there is no need or excuse for punishing her mistakes. Your job is to take the dog to the potty area just before she needs to go, especially with pups under 3 months old. If you aren't watching your pup closely enough and she has an accident, don't punish the puppy for your failure to anticipate her needs. It's not the pup's fault; it's yours.

In any case, punishment is not an effective tool for housetraining most dogs. Many will react to punishment by hiding puddles and feces where you won't find them right away (like behind the couch or under the desk). This eventually may lead to punishment after the fact, which leads to more hiding, and so on.

Instead of punishing for mistakes, stay a step ahead of potty accidents by learning to anticipate your pup's needs. Accompany your dog to the designated potty area when she needs to go. Tell her what you want her to do and praise her when she goes. This will work wonders. Punishment won't be necessary if you are a good teacher.

What happens if you come upon a mess after the fact? Some trainers say a dog can't remember having

It's not fair to expect your baby puppy to be able to control herself the way an adult dog can.

eliminated, even a few moments after she has done so. This is not true. The fact is that urine and feces carry a dog's unique scent, which she (and every other dog) can instantly recognize. So, if you happen upon a potty mistake after the fact you can still use it to teach your dog.

But remember, no punishment! Spanking, hitting, shaking, or scaring a puppy for having a housetraining accident is confusing and counterproductive. Spend your energy instead on positive forms of teaching.

Take your pup and a paper towel to the mess. Point to the urine or feces and calmly tell your puppy, "no potty here." Then scoop or sop up the accident with the paper towel. Take the evidence and the pup to the approved potty area. Drop the mess on the ground and tell the dog, "good potty here," as if she had done the deed in the right place. If your pup sniffs at the evidence, praise her calmly. If the accident happened very recently your dog may not have to go yet, but wait with her a few minutes anyway. If she eliminates, praise her. Afterwards, go finish cleaning up the mess.

Soon the puppy will understand that there is a place where you are pleased about elimination and other places where you are not. Praising for elimination in the approved place will help your pup remember the rules.

Scheduling Basics

With a new puppy in the home, don't be surprised if your rising time is suddenly a little earlier than you've been accustomed to. Puppies have earned a reputation as very early risers. When your pup wakes you at the crack of dawn, you will have to get up and take her to her elimination spot. Be patient. When your dog is an adult, she may enjoy sleeping in as much as you do.

At the end of the chapter, you'll find a typical housetraining schedule for puppies aged 10 weeks to 6 months. (To find schedules for younger and older pups, and for adult dogs, visit this book's companion web site.) It's fine to adjust the rising times when using this schedule, but you should not adjust the intervals between feedings and potty outings unless your pup's behavior justifies a change. Your

Feeding your dog on a regular schedule will make housetraining much easier.

puppy can only meet your expectations in housetraining if you help her learn the rules.

The schedule for puppies is devised with the assumption that someone will be home most of the time with the pup. That would be the best scenario, of course, but is not always possible. You may be able to ease the problems of a latchkey pup by having a neighbor or friend look in on the pup at noon and take her to eliminate. A better solution might be hiring a pet sitter to drop by midday. A professional pet sitter will be knowledgeable about companion animals and can give your pup high-quality care and socialization. Some can even help train your pup in both potty manners and basic obedience. Ask your veterinarian and your dog-owning friends to recommend a good pet sitter.

If you must leave your pup alone during her early housetraining period, be sure to cover the entire floor of her corral with thick layers of overlapping newspaper. If you come home to messes in the puppy corral, just clean them up. Be patient—she's still a baby.

Use this schedule (and the ones on the companion web site) as a basic plan to help prevent housetraining accidents. Meanwhile, use your own powers of observation to discover how to best modify the basic schedule to fit your dog's unique needs. Each dog is an individual and will have her own rhythms, and each dog is reliable at a different age.

Schedule for Pups 10 Weeks to 6 Months

7:00 a.m.	Get up and take the puppy from her sleeping crate to her potty spot.
7:15	Clean up last night's messes, if any.
7:30	Food and fresh water.
7:45	Pick up the food bowl. Take the pup to her potty spot; wait and praise.
8:00	The pup plays around your feet while you have your breakfast.
9:00	Potty break (younger pups may not be able to wait this long).
9:15	Play and obedience practice.
10:00	Potty break.
10:15	The puppy is in her corral with safe toys to chew and play with.

continues

Schedule for Pups 10 Weeks to 6 Months *(continued)*

11:30	Potty break (younger pups may not be able to wait this long).
11:45	Food and fresh water.
12:00 p.m.	Pick up the food bowl and take the pup to her potty spot.
12:15	The puppy is in her corral with safe toys to chew and play with.
1:00	Potty break (younger pups may not be able to wait this long).
1:15	Put the pup on a leash and take her around the house with you.
3:30	Potty break (younger pups may not be able to wait this long).
3:45	Put the pup in her corral with safe toys and chews for solitary play and/or a nap.
4:45	Potty break.
5:00	Food and fresh water.
5:15	Potty break.
5:30	The pup may play nearby (either leashed or in her corral) while you prepare your evening meal.
7:00	Potty break.
7:15	Leashed or closely watched, the pup may play and socialize with family and visitors.
9:15	Potty break (younger pups may not be able to wait this long).
10:45	Last chance to potty.
11:00	Put the pup to bed in her crate for the night.

Appendix

Learning More About Your Boxer

Some Good Books

About the Breed

Abraham, Stephanie, *The Boxer: Family Favorite,* Howell Book House, 2000. (A Dog Writers Association of America award winner!)

Beauchamp, Richard, *Boxers For Dummies,* Wiley Publishing, 2000.

Spitzer, Karla, *The Everything Boxer Book,* Adams Media Corp., 2006.

About Health Care

Arden, Darlene, *The Angell Memorial Animal Hospital Book of Wellness and Preventive Care for Dogs,* McGraw Hill, 2004.

Borzendowski, Janice, *Caring for Your Aging Dog,* Sterling, 2006.

Eldredge, Debra, DVM, Liisa Carlson, DVM, Delbert Carlson, DVM, and James Giffin, MD, *Dog Owner's Home Veterinary Handbook,* 4th ed., Howell Book House, 2007.

Thornton, Kim Campbell, and Debra Eldredge, DVM, *The Everything Dog Health Book,* Adams Media Corp., 2005.

Volhard, Wendy, and Kerry Brown, *Holistic Guide for a Healthy Dog,* Howell Book House, 2000.

About Training

Kilcommons, Brian, and Sarah Wilson, *Good Owners, Great Dogs,* Grand Central Publishing, 1999.
The Monks of New Skete, *The Art of Raising a Puppy,* Little, Brown and Co., 1991.
Smith, Cheryl, *The Rosetta Bone,* Howell Book House, 2004.
Volhard, Jack, and Wendy Volhard, *Dog Training for Dummies,* John Wiley & Sons, 2005.

Dog Sports and Activities

Hall, Lynn, *Dog Showing for Beginners,* Howell Book House, 1994.
O'Neil, Jacqueline, *All About Agility,* Howell Book House, 1999.
Simmons-Moake, Jane, *Excelling at Dog Agility,* Flashpaws Productions, 2007.
Strickland, Winifred, *Expert Obedience Training for Dogs,* 4th ed., Howell Book House, 2003.
Sundance, Kyra, and Chalcy, *101 Dog Tricks,* Quarry Books, 2007.
Zink, M. Christine, DVM, PhD, *Peak Performance: Coaching the Canine Athlete,* Canine Sports Productions, 1997.

Magazines

AKC Gazette
American Kennel Club
260 Madison Ave.
New York, NY 10016
www.akc.org/pubs

The Boxer Ring
P.O. Box 128
Edwardsville, IL 62025
Theboxerring.com

Dog Fancy
P.O. Box 37185
Boone, IA 50037-0185
www.dogfancy.com

Dog Watch
P.O. Box 420235
Palm Coast, FL 32142-0235
www.vet.cornell.edu/publicresources/dog.htm

Dog World
P.O. Box 37185
Boone, IA 50037-0185
www.dogworldmag.com

Clubs and Registries

American Boxer Club
Sandy Orr, Secretary
7106 N. 57th St.
Omaha, NE 68152
www.americanboxerclub.org
This is the national club for the breed; its web site has a great deal of information, including breeder and rescue referrals and lists of upcoming shows and competitions. There are also many all-breed, individual breed, canine sport, and other special-interest dog clubs across the country. The registries listed below can help you find clubs in your area.

American Kennel Club
260 Madison Ave.
New York, NY 10016
(212) 696-8200
www.akc.org

Canadian Kennel Club
89 Skyway Ave.
Suite 100
Etobicoke, Ontario
Canada M9W 6R4
(800) 250-8040 or (416) 675-5511
www.ckc.ca

United Kennel Club
100 E. Kilgore Rd.
Kalamazoo, MI 49002-5584
(269) 343-9020
www.ukcdogs.com

Internet Resources

Boxers

American Boxer Charitable Foundation
www.abcfoundation.org
The ABCF is dedicated to research and fundraising for health issues that affect the Boxer.

American Boxer Club Publications and Videos
www.americanboxerclub.org/order.html
Includes *Meet the Boxer,* 2006, an ideal introduction to the breed.

ABC Regional Clubs
www.americanboxerclub.org/us-boxer-clubs.html
The ABC has approximately 60 member clubs across the nation. You can find out about them here. This is also an ideal site for breeder referral contacts.

ABC Rescue Resources
www.americanboxerclub.org/boxersitesrescue.html
Boxer rescue organizations in the United States are listed here.

The Boxer Underground
www.boxerunderground.com
A great online magazine for Boxer lovers.

Canine Health

American Boxer Club—Boxer Health Information Index
www.americanboxerclub.org/healthtbc.html
Breed-specific health information from the national breed club.

American Veterinary Medical Association
www.avma.org
The American Veterinary Medical Association web site has a wealth of information for dog owners.

Canine Health Information Center
www.caninehealthinfo.org
This centralized canine health database is jointly sponsored by the AKC/Canine Health Foundation and the Orthopedic Foundation for Animals.

Dog Sports and Activities

About.com: Dogs
dogs.about.com/od/activitiesandsports/Sports_Shows_and_Recreation.htm
Lots of articles and links to information on canine sports and competitions.

Dog Patch
www.dogpatch.org
Information on many different dog sports and activities, including conformation shows, agility, and Frisbee.

Dog Play
www.dog-play.com
More about dog sports and activities, including hiking, backpacking, therapy dog work, and much more.

Photo Credits:
Stephanie Abraham: 1, 68, 69, 94, 122, 131
Courtesy of Stephanie Abraham: 21, 22, 24
Bonnie Nance: 4–5, 8–9, 18, 29, 30, 32, 33, 38, 40–41, 46, 61, 63, 73, 129
Isabelle Francais: 11, 13, 17, 19, 27, 34, 36, 39, 42, 43, 50, 51, 52, 53, 55, 59, 64, 65, 68, 75, 78, 80, 81, 83, 88, 89, 90, 98, 100–101, 102, 124, 125, 128, 130, 132
Kent Dannen: 16, 47, 82, 92, 95
Howell Book House: 10

Index